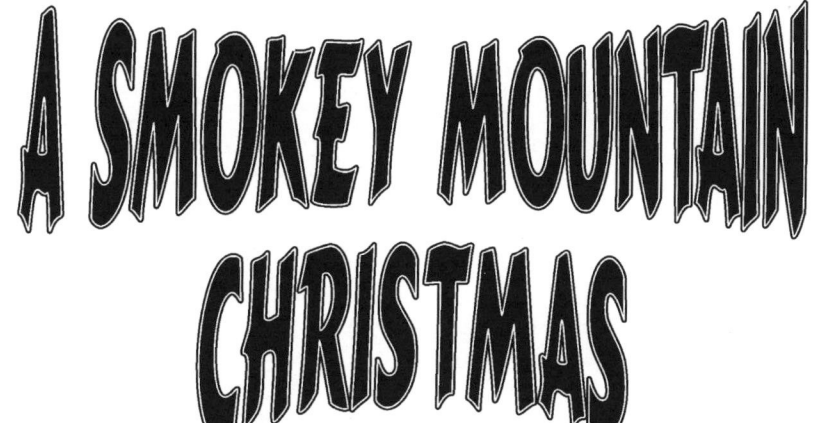

BY STEVE KAUFMAN

www.melbay.com/95474BCDEB

AUDIO CONTENTS

1	Hark the Herald Angels Sing [1:55]	13	Angels We Have Heard on High [2:07]
2	Silent Night [2:55]	14	What Child Is This? [2:44]
3	God Rest Ye Merry Gentlemen [2:09]	15	Deck the Halls [1:04]
4	O' Christmas Tree [3:39]	16	Once in Royal David's City [:57]
5	It Came Upon a Midnight Clear [2:43]	17	O Little Town of Bethlehem [2:02]
6	Go Tell It on the Mountain [1:16]	18	Joy to the World [1:27]
7	The First Noel [2:52]	19	Auld Lang Syne [2:08]
8	We Three Kings [2:42]	20	The Golden Carol [1:05]
9	O Come All Ye Faithful [1:59]	21	Star in the East [1:39]
10	In the Bleak Midwinter [2:16]	22	Down in Yon Forest [1:16]
11	Bring a Torch, Jeanette, Isabella [1:28]	23	And the Trees Do Moan [2:32]
12	Away in a Manger [1:55]	24	While Shepherd's Watched Their Flocks [1:15]

1 2 3 4 5 6 7 8 9 0

© 1995 BY MEL BAY PUBLICATIONS, INC., PACIFIC, MO 63069.
ALL RIGHTS RESERVED. INTERNATIONAL COPYRIGHT SECURED. B.M.I. MADE AND PRINTED IN U.S.A.
No part of this publication may be reproduced in whole or in part, or stored in a retrieval system, or transmitted in any form
or by any means, electronic, mechanical, photocopy, recording, or otherwise, without written permission of the publisher.

Visit us on the Web at www.melbay.com — E-mail us at email@melbay.com

CONTENTS

Introduction 3
About the Author 4
Understanding Your Rhythm Or Back-up Job 5
Reading the Chord Charts 6
Understanding the Notation and Tablature 9
Types of Notes 10
All of the Notes on the Mandolin 13
    And the Trees Do Moan 100
    Angels We Have Heard on High 62
    Auld Lang Syne 86
    Away In A Manger 58
    Bring A Torch, Jeanette, Isabella 54
    Deck The Halls 70
    Down In Yon Forest 98
    The First Noël 38
    Go Tell It On The Mountain 34
    God Rest Ye Merry Gentlemen 22
    The Golden Carol 90
    Hark The Herald Angels Sing 14
    In The Bleak Midwinter 50
    It Came Upon The Midnight Clear 30
    Joy To The World 82
    O Little Town Of Bethlehem 78
    O Christmas Tree (O Tannenbaum) 26
    O Come All Ye Faithful 46
    Once In Royal David's City 74
    Silent Night 18
    Star In The East 94
    What Child Is This? 66
    We Three Kings Of Orient Are 42
    While Shepherds Watched Their Flocks 104
Pointers and Tips 107
Steve Kaufman's Discography 112
For Your Instructional Needs 112

INTRODUCTION

Welcome to my second Christmas book for Mel Bay Publications. The first book is also called *Smokey Mountain Christmas*, but it's for guitarists. It's my pleasure to bring my first Mel Bay Publications Mandolin book to you. The design of this instructional book is multifaceted. It was written and recorded in order to:

A) Make it easy for you to learn these great Christmas songs.

B) Teach you the simple melodies to these tunes on the mandolin.

C) Teach you or another musician how to play the rhythm on the guitar. The guitar back up techniques covered in this manual include hammer-ons, pull-offs and bass walks. The mandolin back up parts are discussed in the first section of the book and should pose no problem to any of mandolin pickers. Any of the techniques covered in this book can and should be used for many different tunes as long as they follow the same chord structure.

E) Provide you with an intermediate/advanced solo that is comprised of melodic embellishments and standard runs that can also be inserted into other songs that use the same chord structure (this is a technique that sounds easier than it really is).

I have recorded the basic melody as it is written, then the intermediate version, then I follow that with an improvised version on either the guitar or the mandolin. The reason for this extra improvised solo is to give you a chance to hear how runs and licks are interchangeable. At some point you may hear the runs and licks from one tune found in another tune. Eventually you will see how they fit together in other songs. Practice this technique of patching together solos from runs and licks out of different songs. When you get it down, you will never have to say that you don't know or can't play the song.

Special thanks to Bill Bay and Mel Bay Publications for teaching the world and for helping me get my work out to you. Thanks to Claudio and Susan Tolaini for their support over the years – Merry Christmas. Thanks to my brother Mike for his song suggestions of "In The Bleak Mid Winter" and "Once In Royal David's City." Once again, thanks to Mr. Eugene McCammon for helping me out with some of the words to these songs.

Special thanks to all of you reading this now. It makes me very proud to hear my arrangements being played as I travel around the world. You are all doing a great job keeping this music style alive – so to you I say thanks!

Be sure to work through my other instructional books and videos. They are all different but tie together in some way. They don't repeat any versions or arrangements and they will make you a better picker.

Please feel free to write to me with any specific questions you may have or call my 1-800-FLATPIK number and I or someone from my staff will get back in touch with you. I usually keep a small stack of mail on my desk but I will eventually get back to you, so please be patient.

Good luck and have fun with this book.

Merry Christmas and Happy Holidays!
Best Always,

Steve Kaufman

Steve Kaufman

ABOUT THE AUTHOR

Steven S. Kaufman was born April 20, 1957, in New York City. He was introduced to music by his father, a jazz pianist, and his mother, a classically trained pianist. At the age of four, Steve started to play the piano and later moved on to the cello. At 10 , he began playing the guitar, but after a few years of strumming, he put the guitar under the bed. At 14, Steve started "picking" the guitar and he has not put it down since.

Steve is the only three-time winner of the prestigious National Flatpicking Championships held in Winfield, Kansas, capturing 1st place in 1978, 1984 and 1986. His music covers a broad range of styles including bluegrass favorites, popular swing standards, Irish and Appalachian fiddle tunes, folk and country classics and novelty tunes. Steve has been pleasing crowds from California to Austria since 1976, performing in a wide variety of settings from elementary schools and colleges, to major bluegrass festivals and concerts.

Steve keeps busy writing instructional manuals for Mel Bay Publications plus audio and video instructional material for Homespun Tapes. He also has an extensive recording career, performance and workshop touring agenda and a full schedule of private students in Maryville, Tennessee.

UNDERSTANDING YOUR RHYTHM OR BACK-UP JOB

The rhythm person is the backbone of the group. He or she must be steady and true. But keep in mind that the rhythm or back-up person is just that — a back-up player. You should be aware that it doesn't take much volume or power to be heard. **Do not play too loudly,** lest you drown out the singers or other pickers. Play the back-up role. *You should be heard but not overheard.*

There are two basic types of time signatures for most western music – 3/4 time and 4/4 time. Let's look at 3/4 time first. This simply means that there are three beats in every measure. This translates into rhythm terms as three strums per measure or a rest and two strums or an accented or heavy first strum with two lighter strums to follow or a strum then a rest then another strum. The combinations are almost endless as long as each measure consists of only three beats. Examples of some of the 3/4 time songs within this book are: "What Child Is This," "Silent Night," "The First Noël," "It Came Upon The Midnight Clear," "We Three Kings," and "Away In A Manger." All 3/4 time songs move quite quickly. The rest of the songs in this book are in 4/4 time so they will have four beats in all of the measures. The same rhythm rules would apply as with 3/4 time except add one more strum or rest. So to recap 3/4 and 4/4 rhythm patterns – the standard 3/4 pattern would be: Rest-Strum-Strum; and a standard 4/4 time pattern would be: Rest-Strum-Rest-Strum.

These patterns take lots of practice to play smoothly. Practice along with the recording. It is very difficult in the beginning to keep a steady beat. Keep one thing in mind as you practice the rhythm sections – you can only play as fast as you can change the chords. This means if it takes two seconds to change from a G chord to a C chord, then there should be the same two second gap between everything in the song. Count "1, 2, 3, 4" for each beat and be sure to hit a strum on its correlating number.

Reading the Chord Charts

The following chord charts show how to hold most of the basic chords. My chord charts are laid out as if you were holding the mandolin straight out in front of you looking at the strings. The peghead is at the top and the end pin at the bottom. The first, or top, horizontal black line represents the nut. The vertical lines going up and down represent the strings, and the horizontal lines going across represent the frets. The dots represent your fingertips on the frets that need to be held. Notice the placement of the dots. They are right up against the fret. *Be sure to place your fingers as close to the frets as possible. The farther away from the fret, the harder it is to push and get a clear note.* Familiarize yourself with the chords and refer back to these charts throughout the series.

Some Chords You'll Need To Know

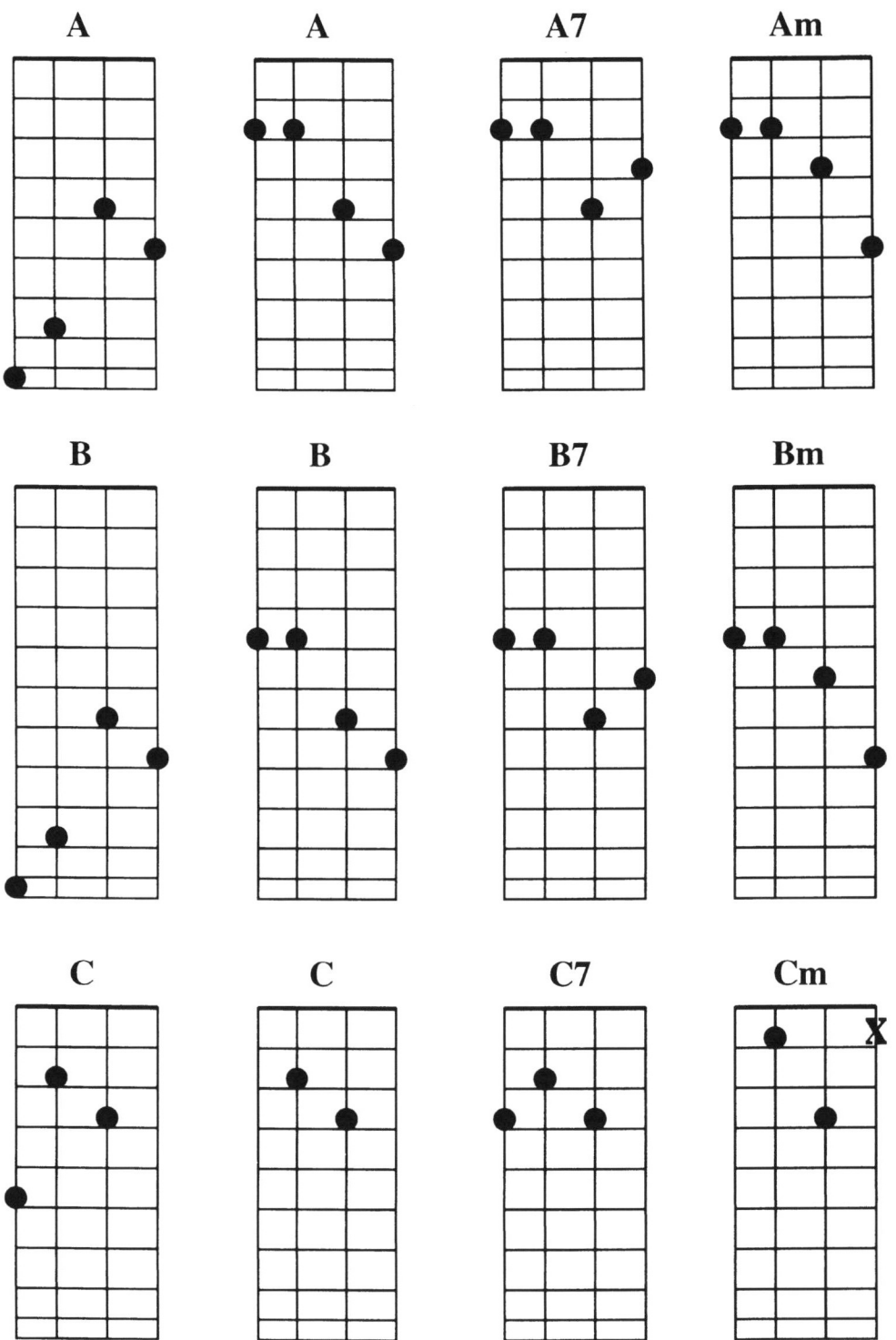

Some Chords You'll Need To Know

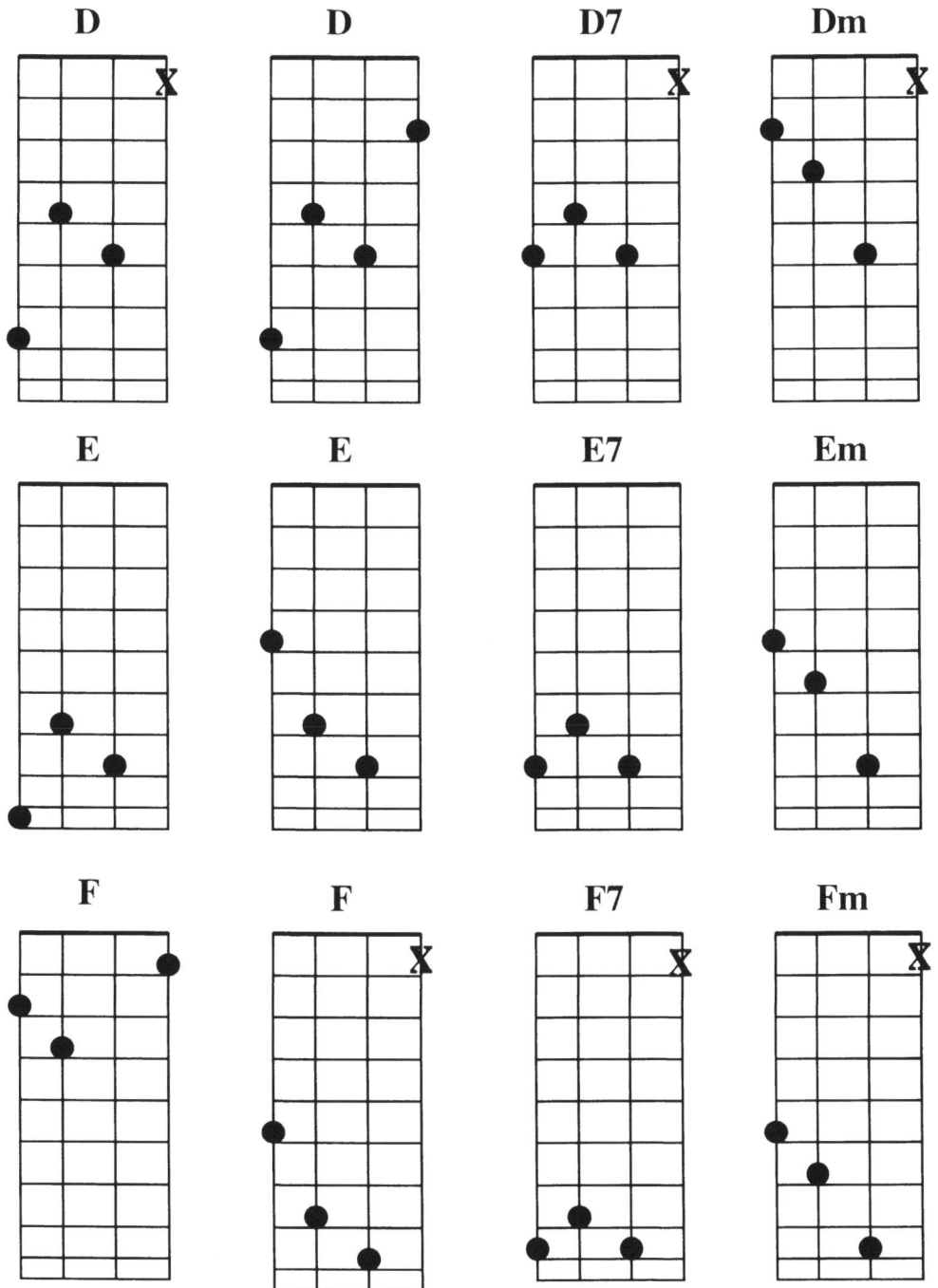

Some Chords You'll Need To Know

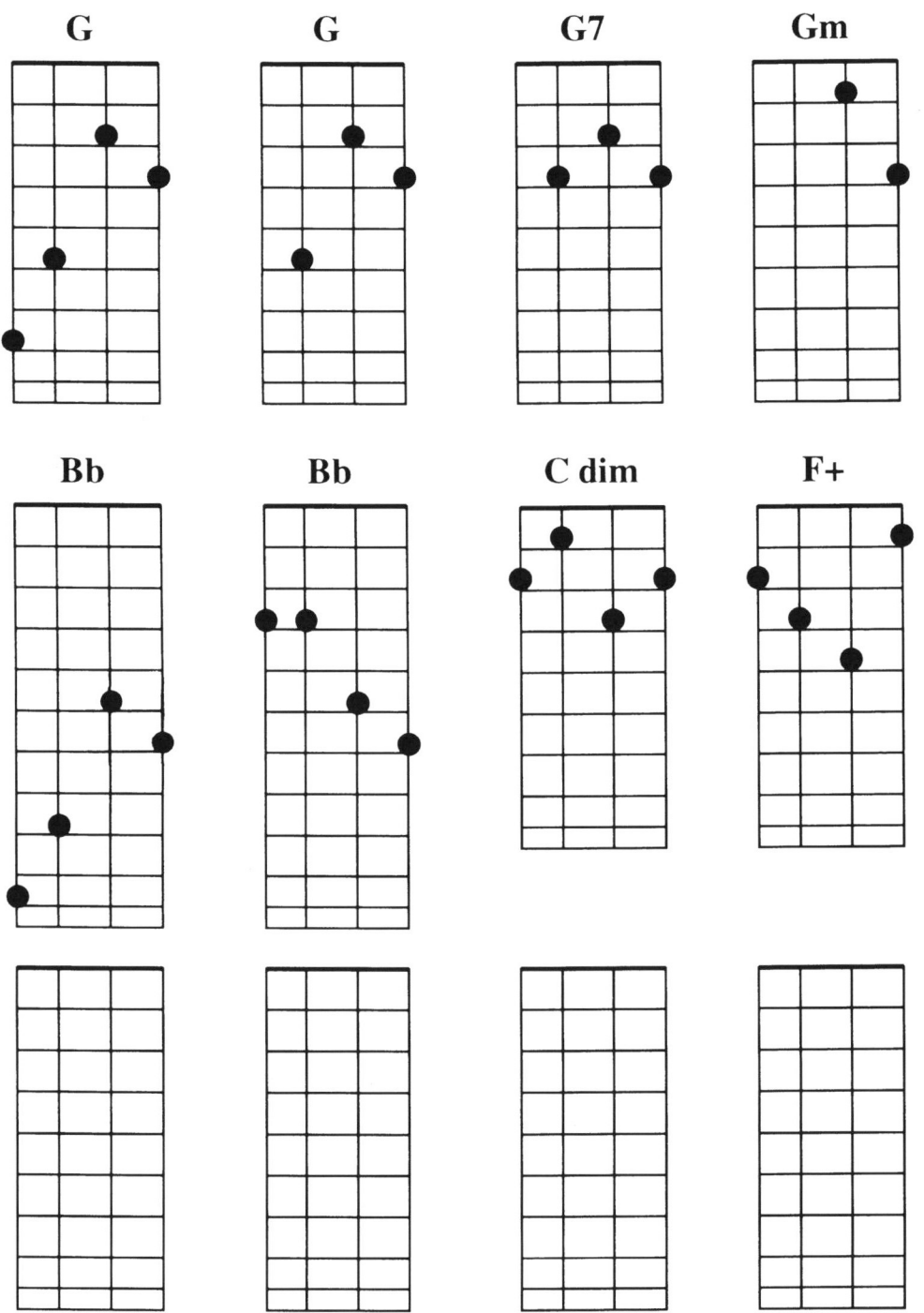

UNDERSTANDING THE NOTATION AND TABLATURE

Notes on the Strings

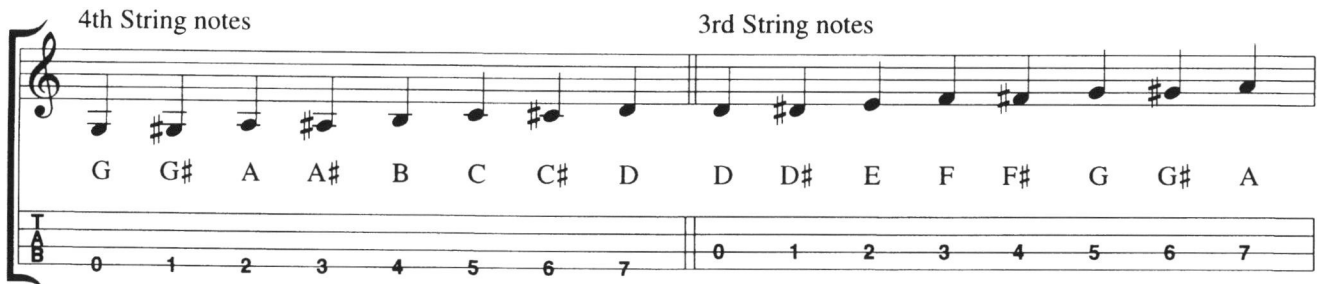

TYPES OF NOTES

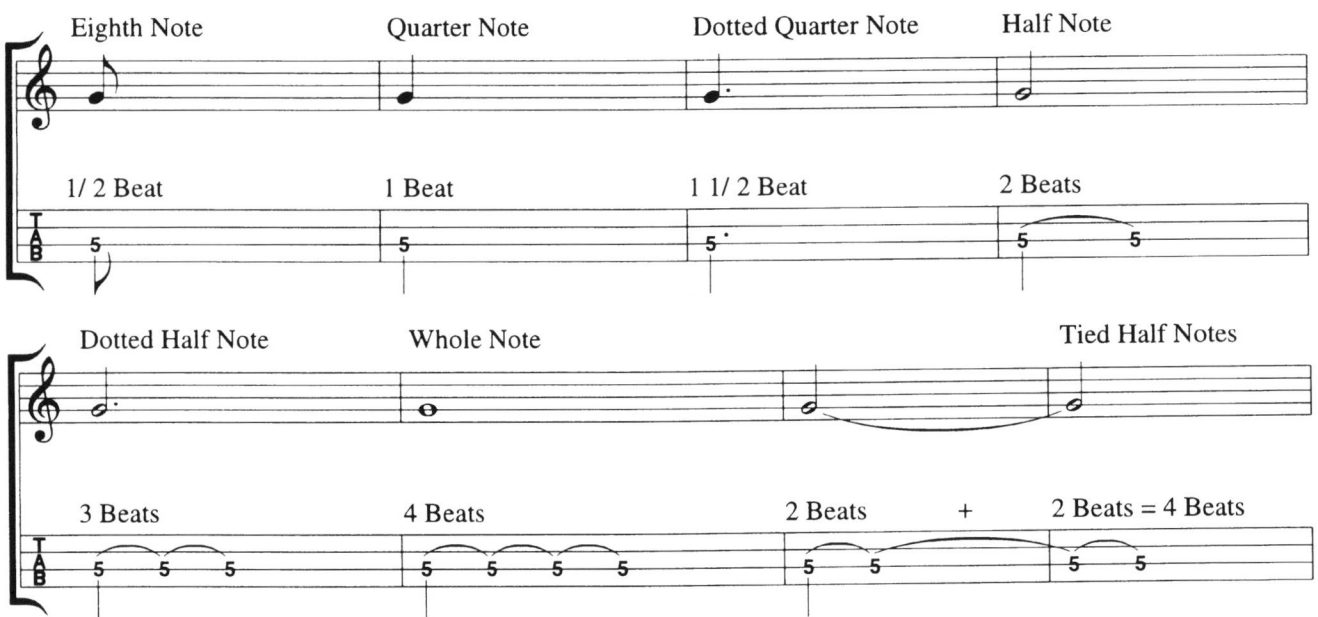

These notes are all G notes (third string open). They represent different lengths of time or different amounts of beats.

The first note is an **eighth note** (1/8). It is called an "eighth note" because it would take eight of these notes to make up a whole measure. A measure is bordered by two vertical lines. Look at the following exercise. It is made up of eight measures. Count the boxes that are made up of eight measures. Count the boxes that are made up of the vertical lines, and these are called the "measures." The eighth note will last half of a beat and, in my tab/note system, if there is only one eighth note, it is hit with an up swing going directly to the next note on a down swing.

The next note is a **quarter note** (1/4). It gets a whole beat and is always hit with a down swing. Four quarter notes would fill up a whole measure.

Next is a quarter note with a dot after it, called a **"dotted quarter note."** A dot after a note adds half of the value of the note itself. The quarter note gets one beat—half of that would be half of a beat, so the dotted quarter note gets a total of one and a half (1 1/2) beats. It is hit with a down swing. When a note like this is present, there is a 99% chance that you will find a single eighth note in the same measure.

The next note is a **half note**. It gets 2 beats. If there were four beats in a measure, the half note would take up half of that measure. The tab shows this note tied to another note. A half note also represents 2 beats when tied this way. Hit the note only once and hold it for another beat. It is hit with a down swing.

Next is the **dotted half note**. It lasts for 3 beats, and the tab shows it as a note tied to two others. Hit this note one time and hold it for 2 more beats to make a total of 3 beats. It is hit with a down swing.

The next note is a **whole note**. It lasts for 4 beats and is called a "whole note" because it takes all the time of a measure in 4/4 time—4 beats. The tab shows it as the first note tied to three others. Hit it only once and let it ring for 4 beats. It is hit with a down swing.

Next is a **half note tied to another half note** of the next measure. You must add the time (the number of beats) of the first note to the time of the second note. Adding it all together, this is the number of beats that the note should ring. If you had a dotted half note (3 beats) tied to a quarter note (1 beat), then the note should ring for 4 beats total time. It is hit with a down swing.

Play through the following exercise to get familiar with the notes and the tab. Be sure to watch out for the timing. All the notes are to be hit with a down swing. Play the exercise with the notes first, checking with the first chart to find where the notes are, then go through the exercise using the tab system. Play it backwards and forwards to help familiarize yourself with the notes and the tab. Be sure to play it backwards and forwards. Trust me—I have my reasons.

Play this exercise backwards and forwards:

The next few examples deal with timing. The first measure shows four **quarter notes**. They are all hit with a down swing. On top of each measure is a row of numbers with a "+" between them. When you hit quarter notes or any notes larger than a single eighth note, they are hit on down swings and on the number. To see how this works, count out loud:

1 + 2 + 3 + 4 +

Now hit the notes when you say the numbers. Be sure to count steadily, and don't hit any note on a "+." This is the proper way to hit quarter notes.

The next measure shows **eighth notes**. It doesn't matter whether they are tied (or beamed) together at the bottom or the top or whether they are grouped in sets of two or four. What matters is the right-hand motion with eighth notes. The first eighth note is always hit down, the second is hit up, and so on. Count "1 + 2 + 3 + 4 +," hitting the first note down on the number, the second note up on the "+," down on the number, up on the "+." Keep it steady. There is very little time between eighth notes. They go as fast as you can count and sometimes faster. Tap your foot while you are counting. Notice that your foot goes down on the number and up on the "+." Your right hand moves the same way. Practice eighth notes while counting and tapping your foot.

The fourth measure illustrates **hammer-ons** and **pull-offs**. The hammer-on is marked by a slur or tie over or under the notes. The example shows an open string to the 2nd fret. Hit the open string and, without your right hand hitting the string again, shoot the second finger of your left hand onto the 2nd fret. You must shoot your second finger onto the string very sharply. It doesn't have to be fast—it just has to have a fast attack.

The pull-off is just the opposite. Put your second finger on the 2nd fret of the third string. Hit the third string and, without hitting the string again, pull your finger off the string. It is best to dig under the string a little so you will have a stronger, pluckier pull-off.

The next measure shows a series of eighth notes with hammer-ons and pull-offs. Pay close attention to the arrows and the timing. Be sure to count "1 + 2 + 3 + 4 +," etc., while you practice this exercise.

On either side of this measure are **repeat signs**. They are shown as two vertical lines with two dots. The repeat signs face each other. The first sign tells you that there is another repeat sign coming up soon and, when you get to it, go back to the first sign and play the section over again. In this exercise, play the measure for about two minutes without stopping, just to practice the hammers and pulls.

The next measure deals with **slides**. It is very important when doing a slide to maintain your finger pressure so that the note will ring the entire length of the slide and hopefully a little after the slide has ended. Slides usually involve two notes, as do hammer-ons and pull-offs—the starting point and the ending point. Your right hand hits them only once. Let your left hand do the rest.

Next we have **bends**. Place your third finger on the second string, 3rd fret. This is the note you are going to practice bending. Hit the second string and try to bend, or push the note, to the pitch of the next fret so that the 3rd fret sounds like the 4th fret.

It is difficult to bend the string and hold it for any length of time. The easiest way to bend a note is to put your third finger on the 3rd fret; your second finger on the same string, 2nd fret; and your first finger on the 1st fret, same string. Hit the second string, and push all three fingers up at the same time. Use the combined strength of all three fingers to achieve a smooth bend. Be sure to maintain the finger pressure, or else the note will die off before its time.

The last three measures deal with hammer-ons and slides in groups of eighth notes. By now you know the procedure; just be careful with the down-ups and the timing.

TIMING AND TABLATURE CONT.

ALL OF THE NOTES ON THE MANDOLIN
To The 12th Fret

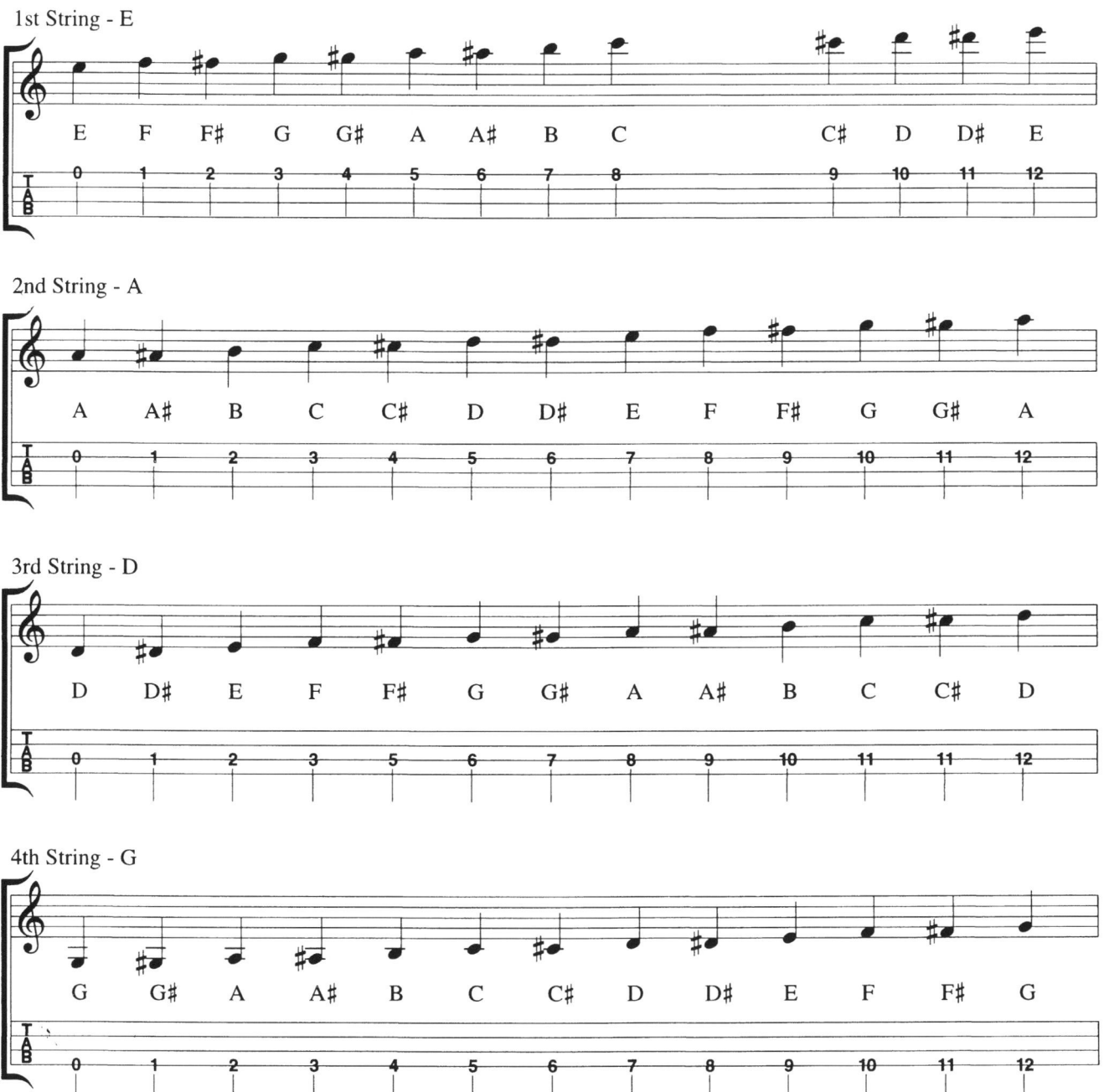

HARK THE HERALD ANGELS SING

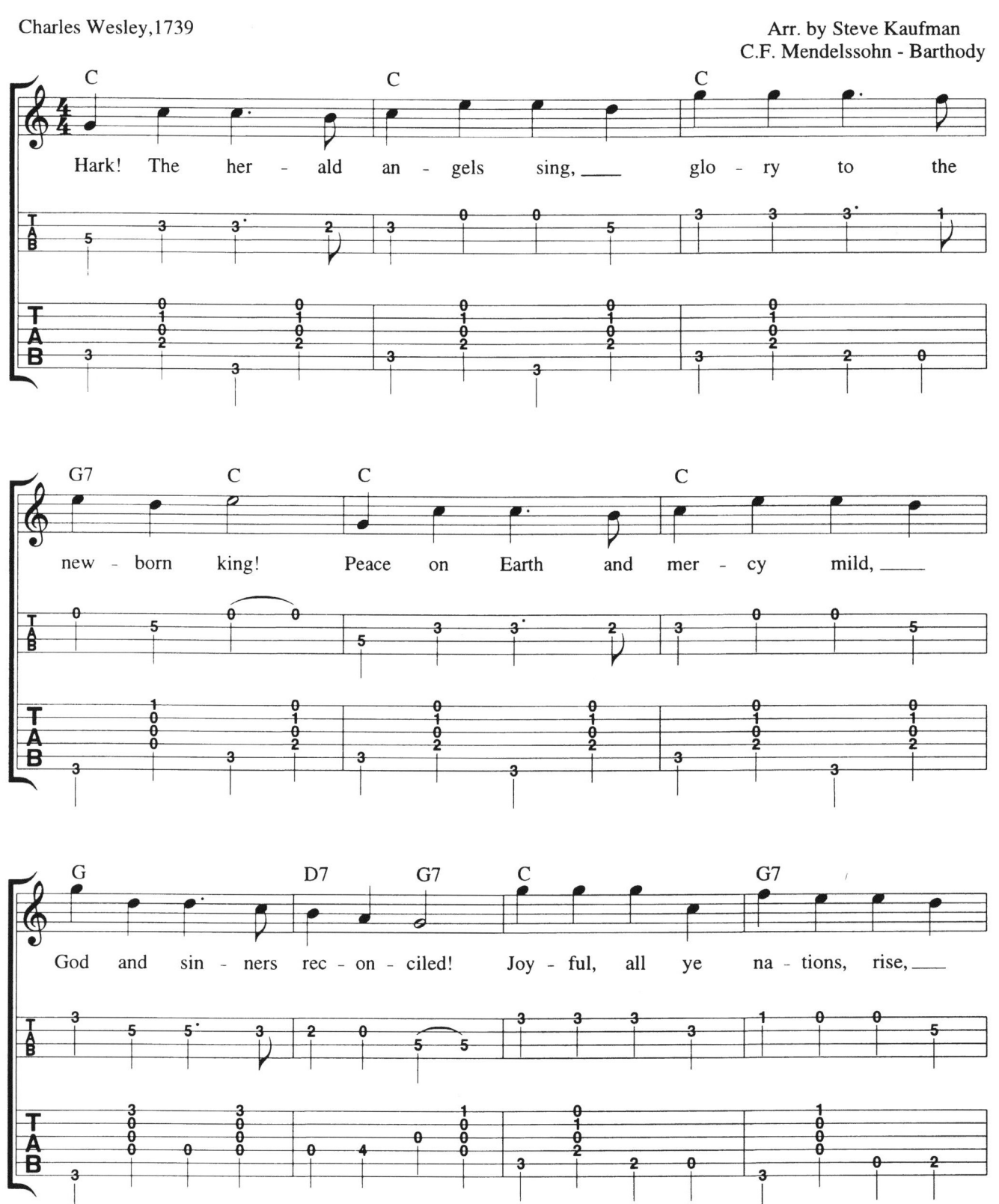

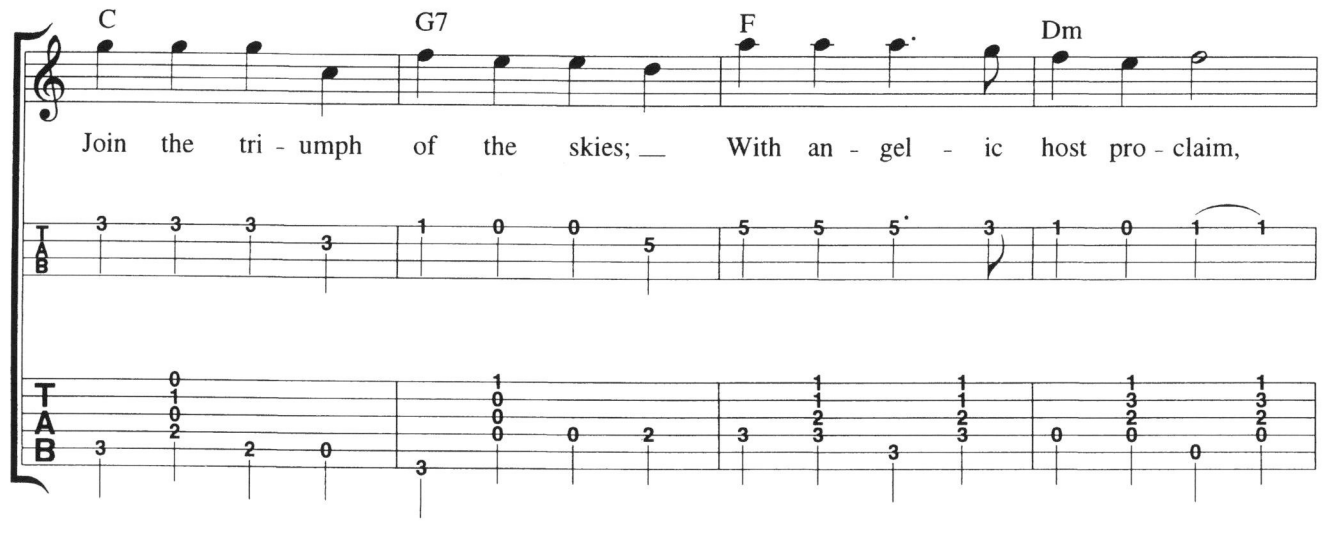
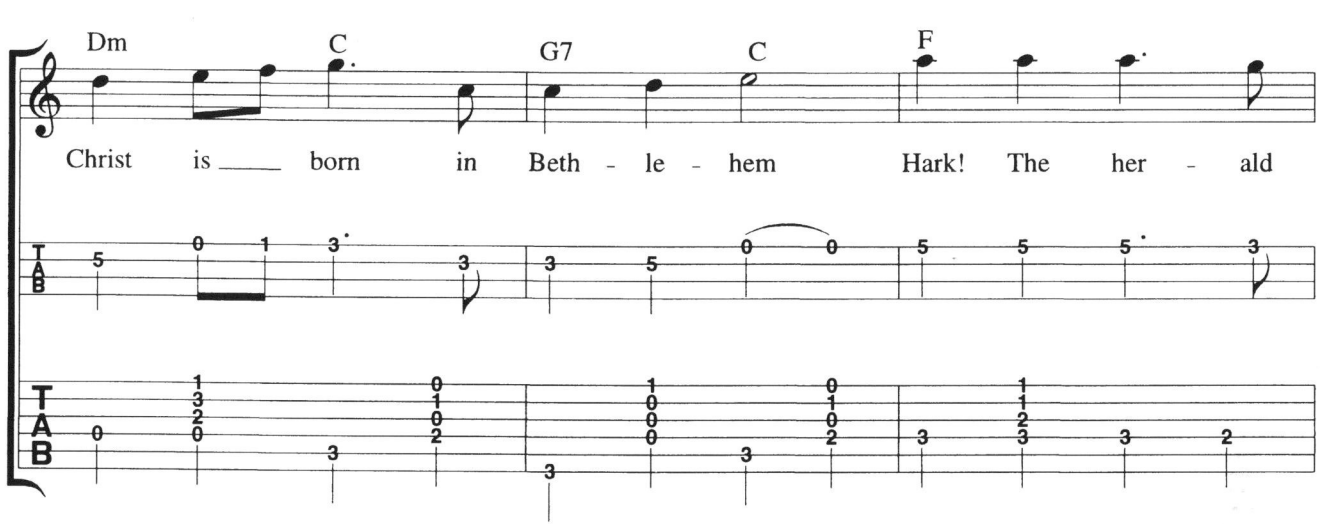
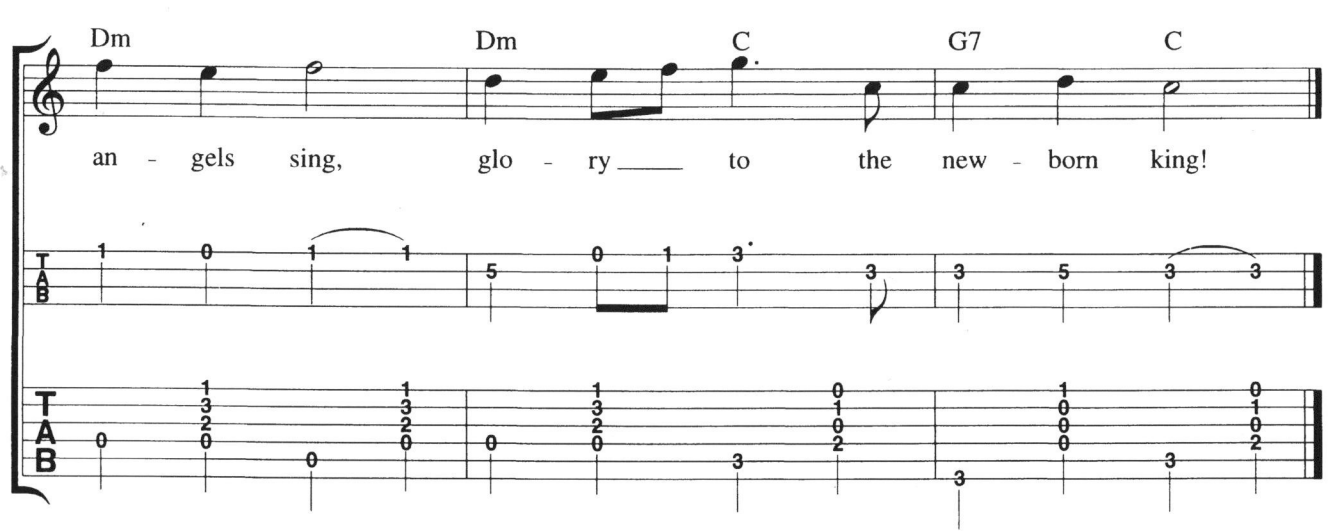

15

HARK THE HERALD ANGELS SING

Arr. by Steve Kaufman

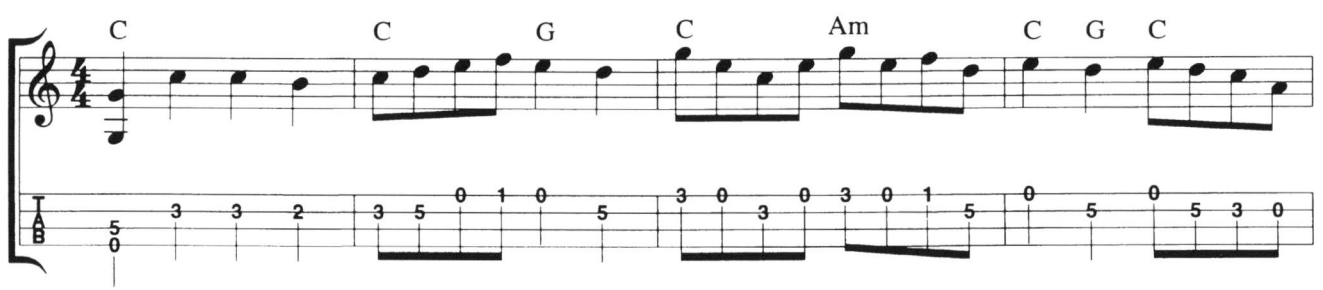
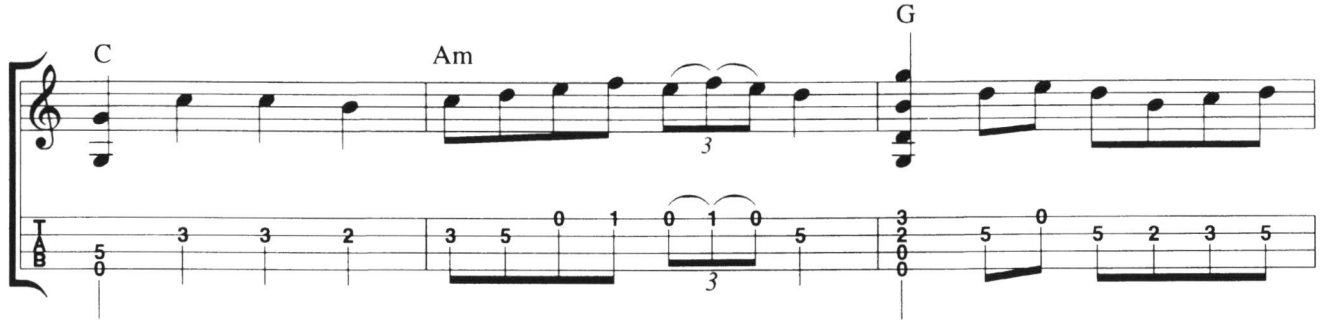
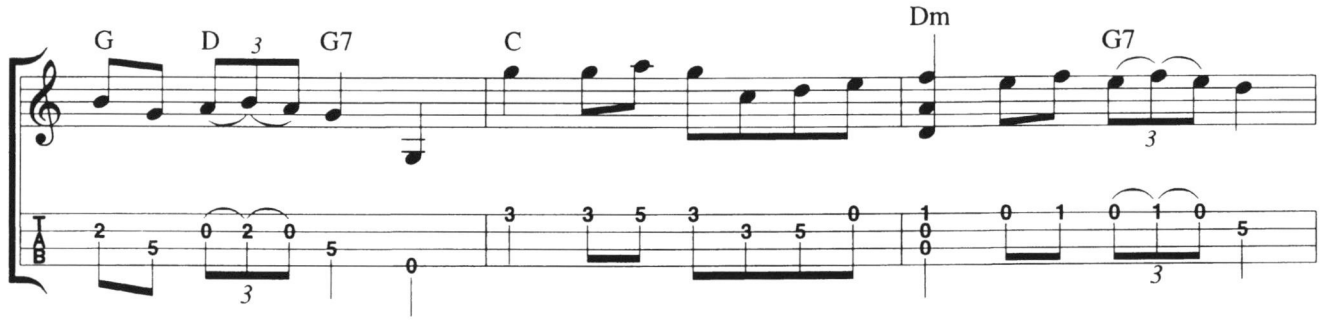
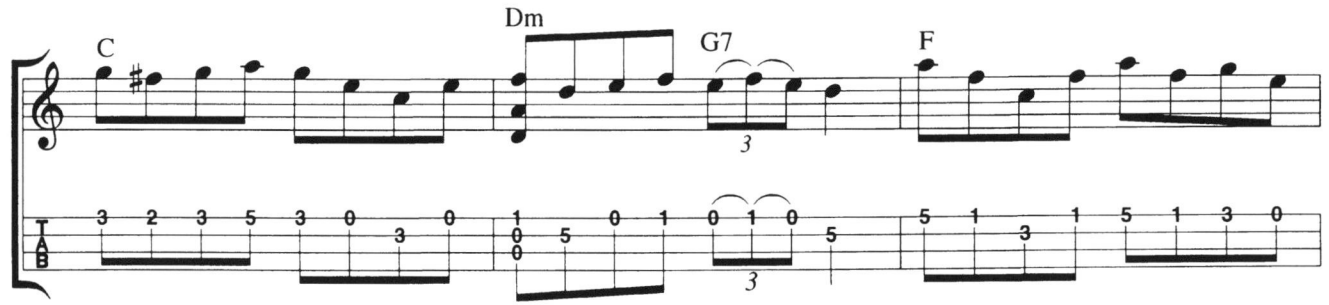

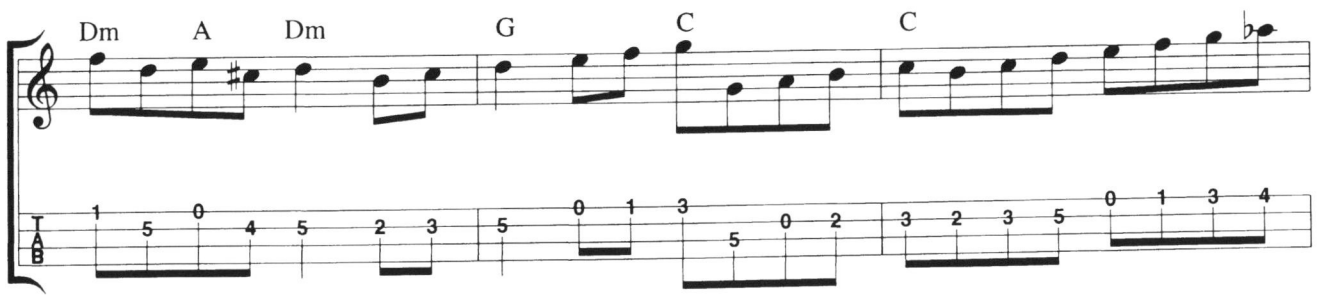

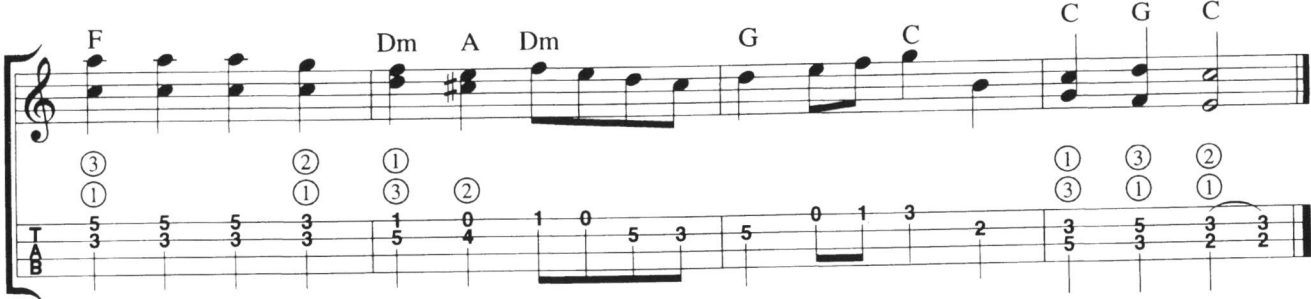

1. Hark! The herald angels sing,
   "Glory to the newborn King;
   Peace on earth and mercy mild;
   God and sinners reconciled!"
   Joyful all ye nations rise;
   Join the triumph of the skies;
   With angelic hosts proclaim,
   "Christ is born in Bethlehem!"
   Hark! The herald angels sing,
   "Glory to the newborn King."

2. Christ, by highest heaven adored;
   Christ the everlasting Lord!
   Long desired, behold Him come,
   Finding here his humble home.
   Veiled in flesh the God-head see;
   Hail the incarnate Deity,
   Pleased as man with men to dwell,
   Jesus our Emmanuel.
   Hark! the herald angels sing,
   "Glory to the newborn King."

3. Hail the heaven born Prince of Peace!
   Hail the Son of Righteousness!
   Light and life to all He brings,
   Risen with healing in his wings.
   Mild He lays his glory by,
   Born that man no more may die,
   Born to raise the sons of earth,
   Born to give them second birth.
   Hark! The herald angels sing,
   "Glory to the newborn King."

   Amen

SILENT NIGHT

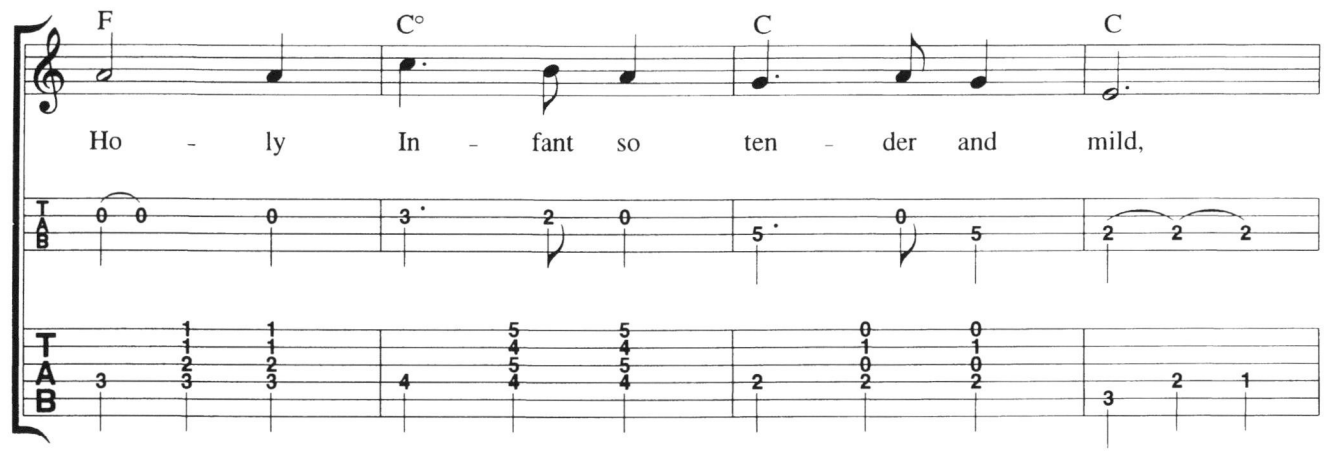

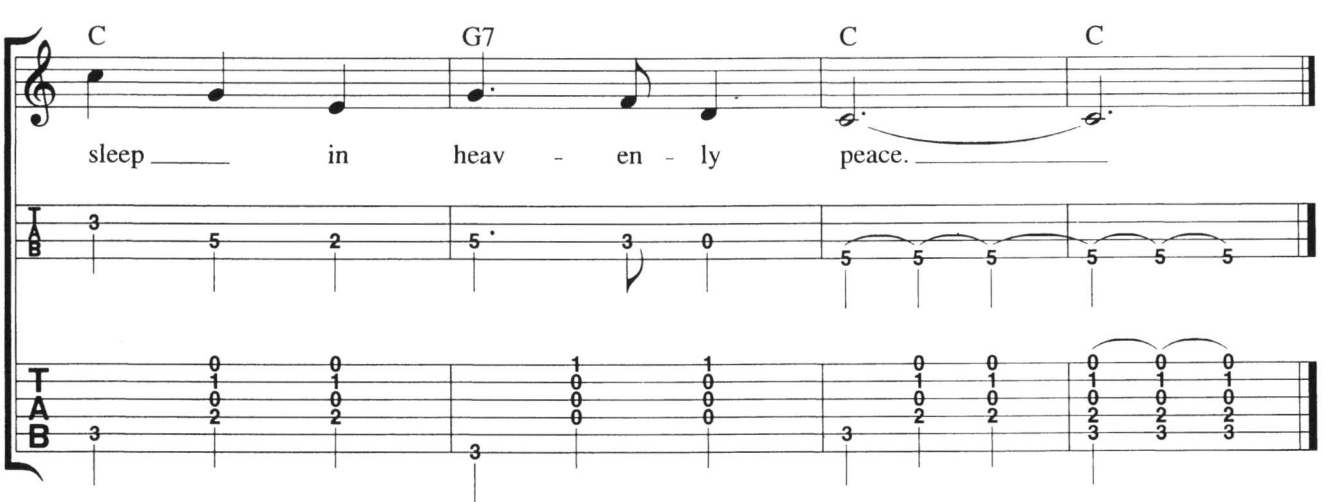

SILENT NIGHT

Arr. by Steve Kaufman

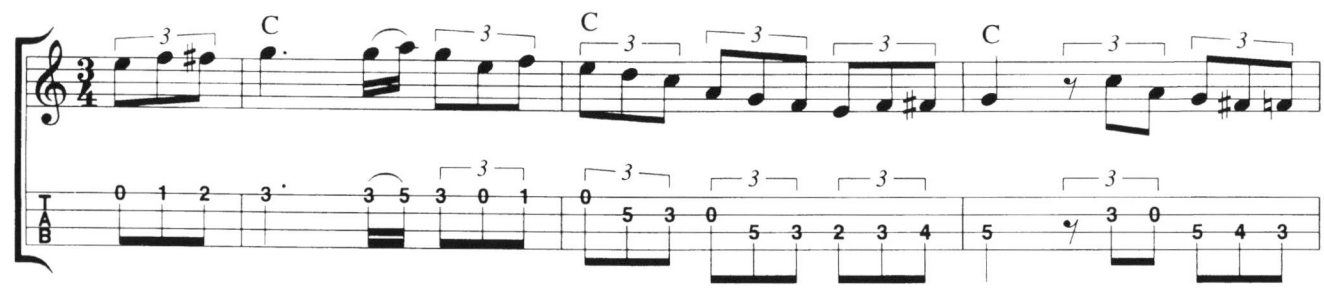
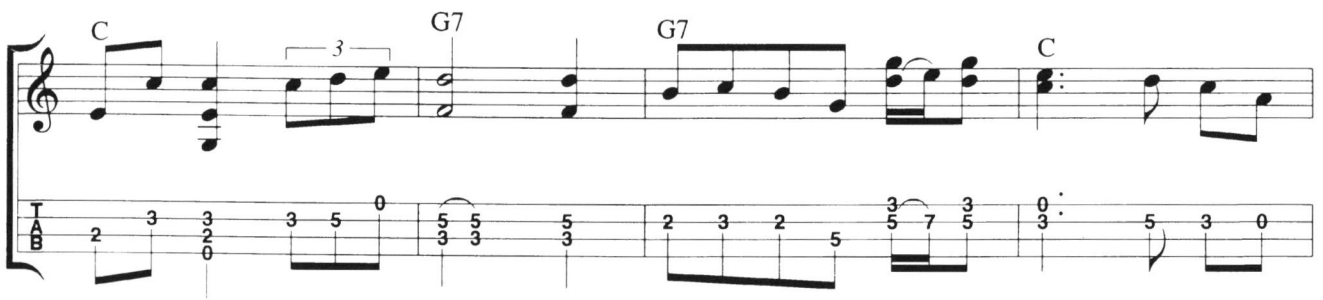
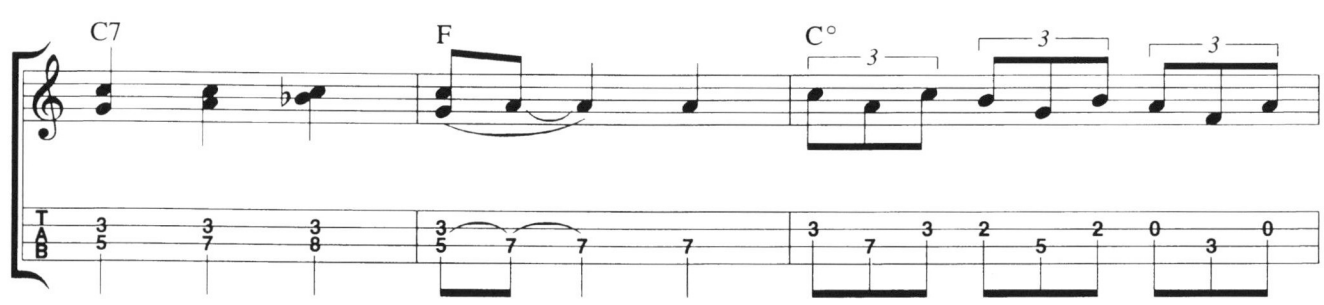

1. Silent night, holy night
   All is calm, all is bright
   Round yon virgin mother and child!
   Holy Infant so tender and mild,
   Sleep in heavenly peace,
   Sleep in heavenly peace.

2. Silent night, holy night,
   Shepherds quake at the sight,
   Glories stream from heaven afar,
   Heavenly hosts sing alleluya;
   Christ the Savior is born!
   Christ the Savior is born!

3. Silent night, holy night,
   Son of God, love's pure light;
   Radiant beams from thy holy face,
   With the dawn of redeeming grace,
   Jesus, Lord, at thy birth,
   Jesus, Lord, at thy birth.

4. Silent night, holy night,
   Wondrous star, lend thy light;
   With the angels let us sing,
   "Alleluia to our King;
   Christ the Savior is born!
   Christ the Savior is born."

   Amen

GOD REST YE MERRY GENTLEMEN

Arr. by Steve Kaufman

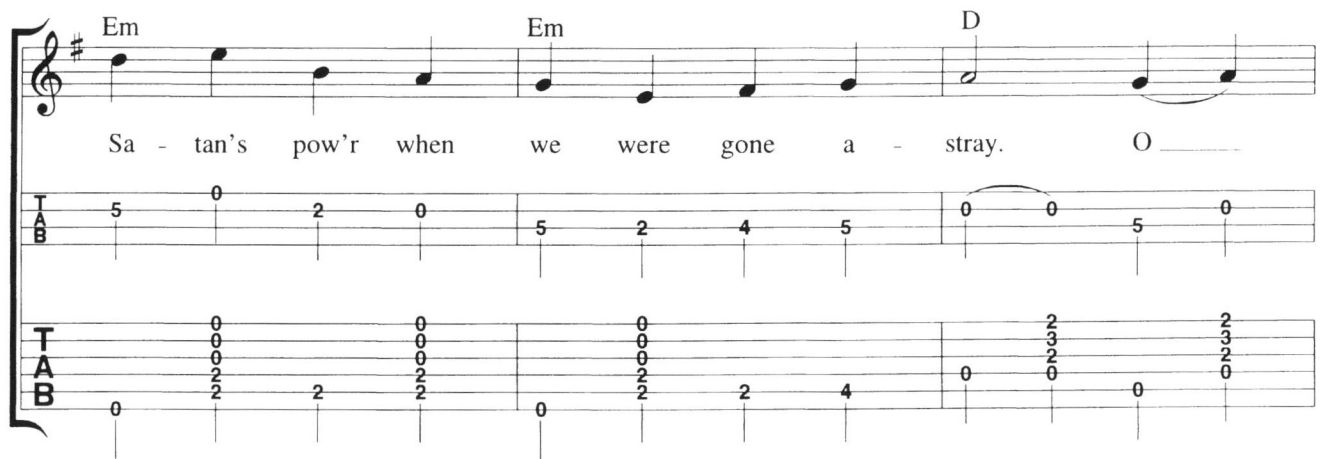
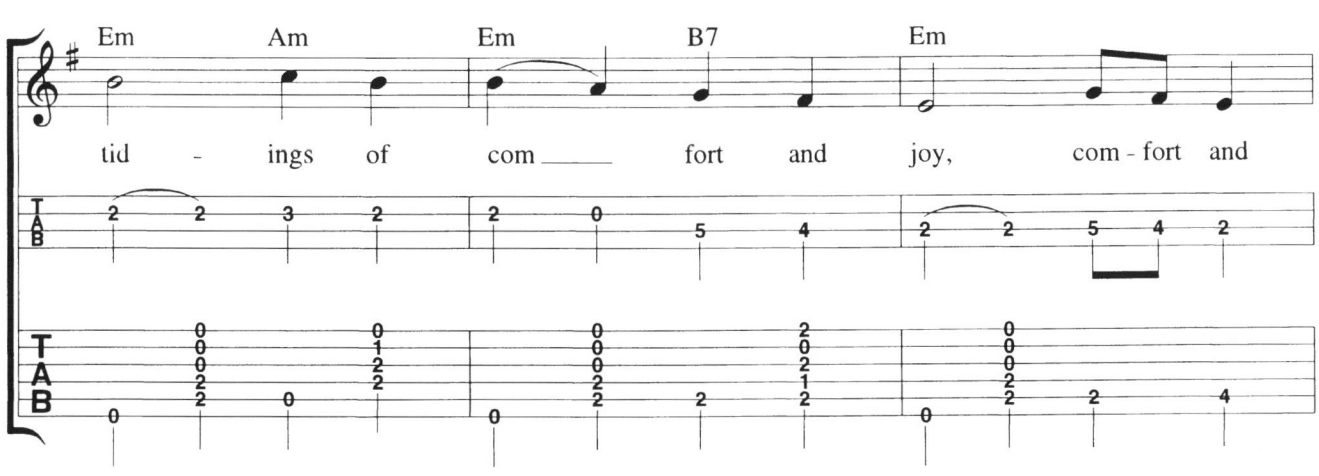
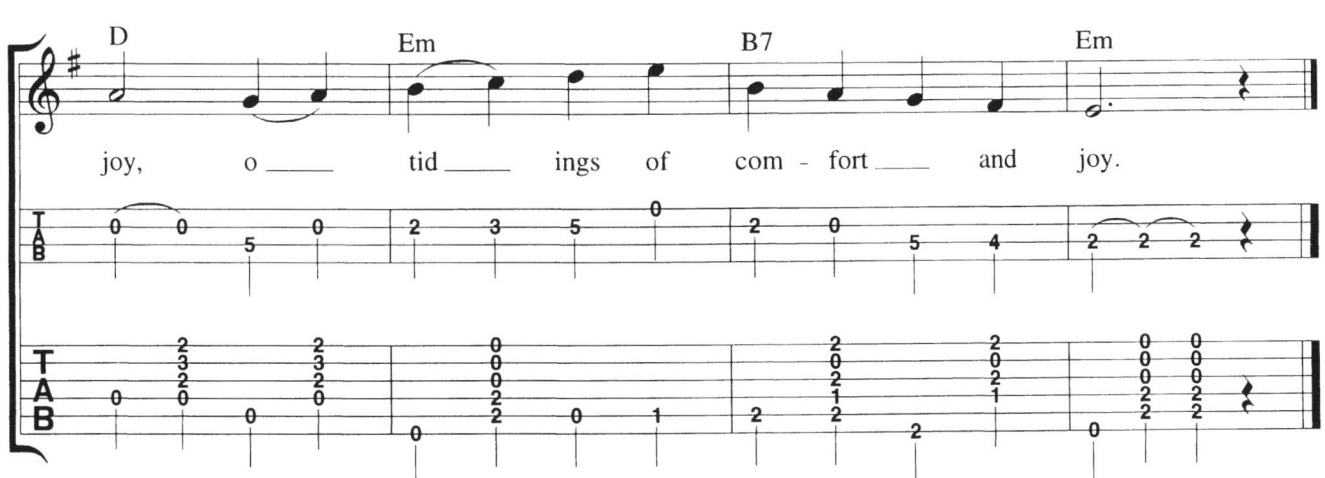

GOD REST YE MERRY GENTLEMEN

Arr. by Steve Kaufman

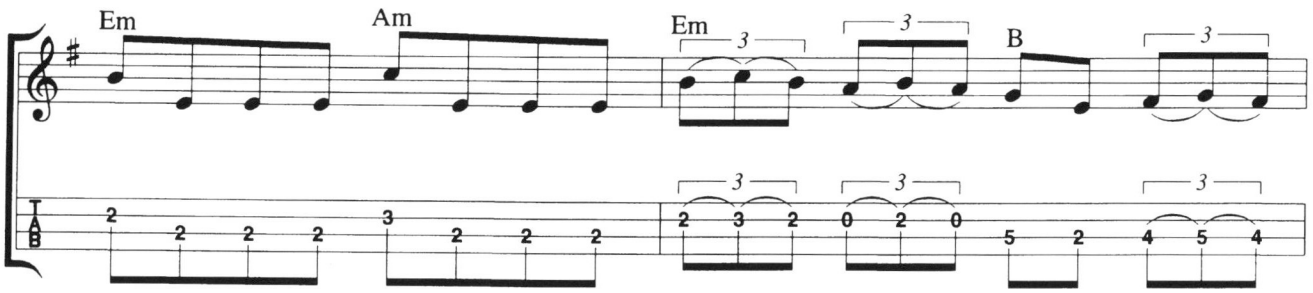

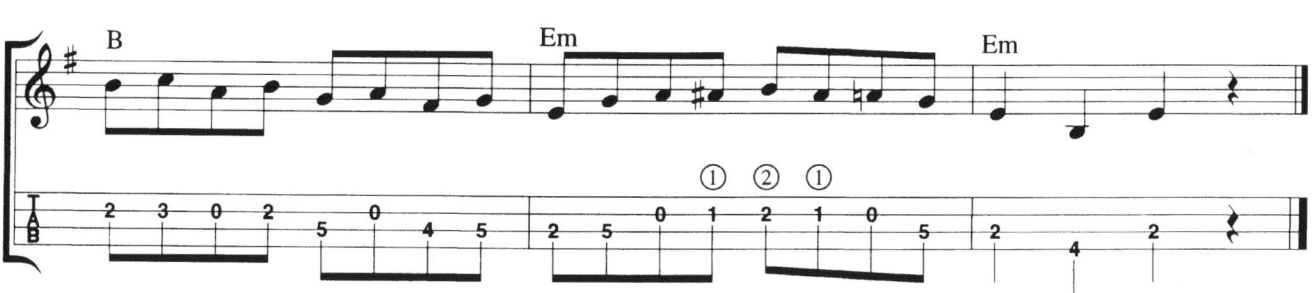

1. God rest you merry, gentlemen,
   Let nothing you dismay,
   For Jesus Christ our savior
   Was born on Christmas day,
   To save us all from Satan's power
   When we were gone astray.
   O tidings of comfort and joy,
   comfort and joy;
   O tidings of comfort and joy.

2. In Bethlehem in Jewry
   This blessed babe was born,
   And laid within a manger
   Upon this blessed morn:
   The which his mother Mary
   Did nothing take in scorn.
   O tidings of comfort and joy,
   comfort and joy;
   O tidings of comfort and joy!

3. From God our heavenly Father
   A blessed angel came,
   And unto certain shepherd
   Brought tidings of the same,
   How that in Bethlehem was born
   The Son of God by name.
   O tidings of comfort and joy,
   comfort and joy;
   O tidings of comfort and joy!

4. The shepherds at those tidings
   Rejoiced much in mind,
   And left their flocks afeeding
   In tempest, storms, and wind,
   And went to Bethlehem straight way,
   The blessed babe to find.
   O tidings of comfort and joy,
   comfort and joy;
   O tidings of comfort and joy!

5. Now to the Lord sing praises,
   All you within this place,
   And with true love and brotherhood
   Each other now embrace;
   This holy tide of Christmas
   All other doth deface.
   O tidings of comfort and joy,
   comfort and joy;
   O tidings of comfort and joy!

O CHRISTMAS TREE
(O Tannenbaum)

Arr. by Steve Kaufman

26

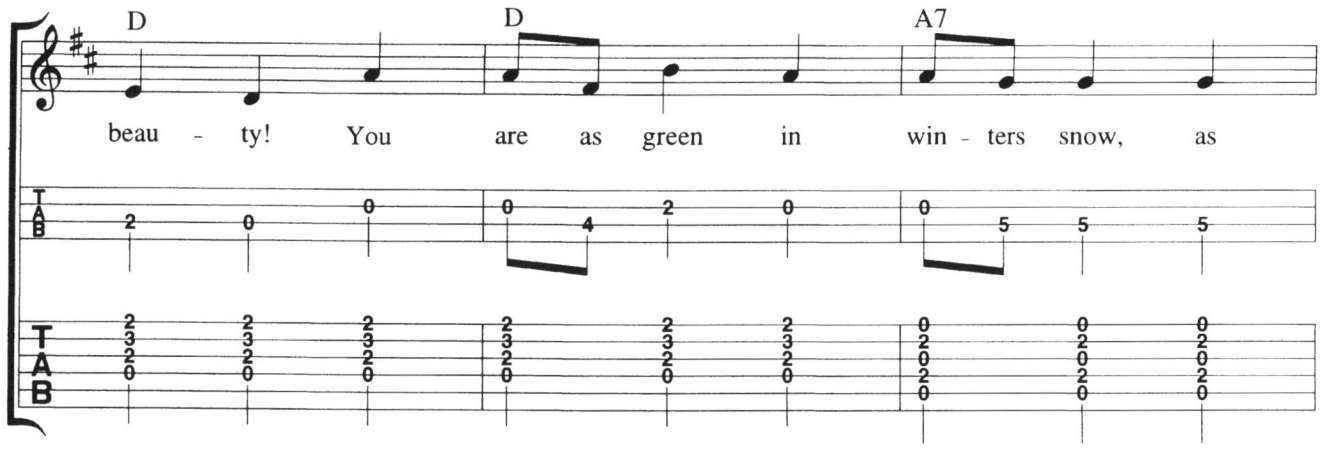
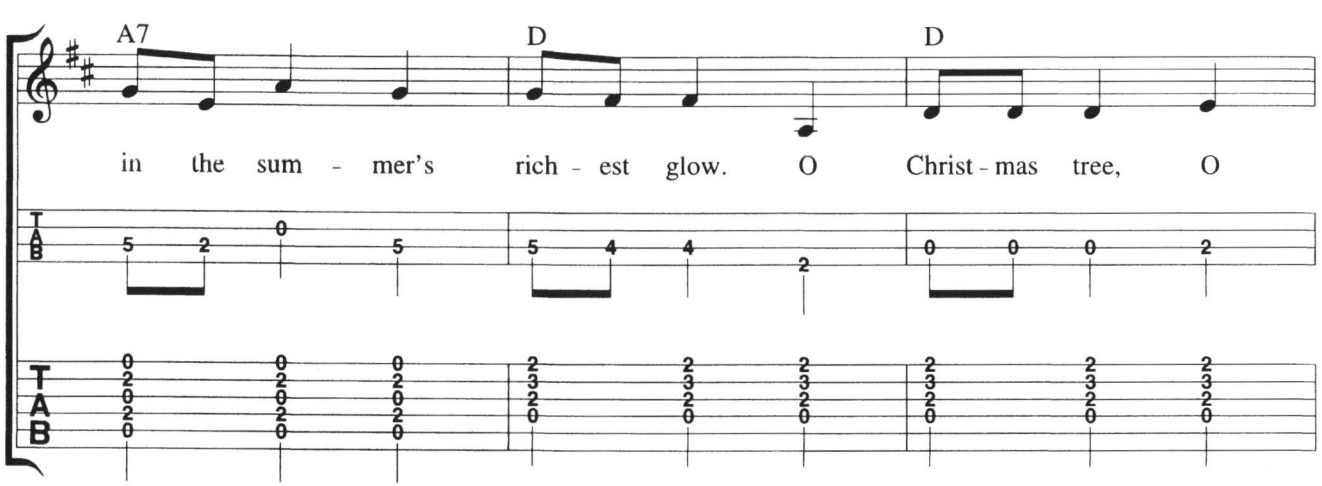
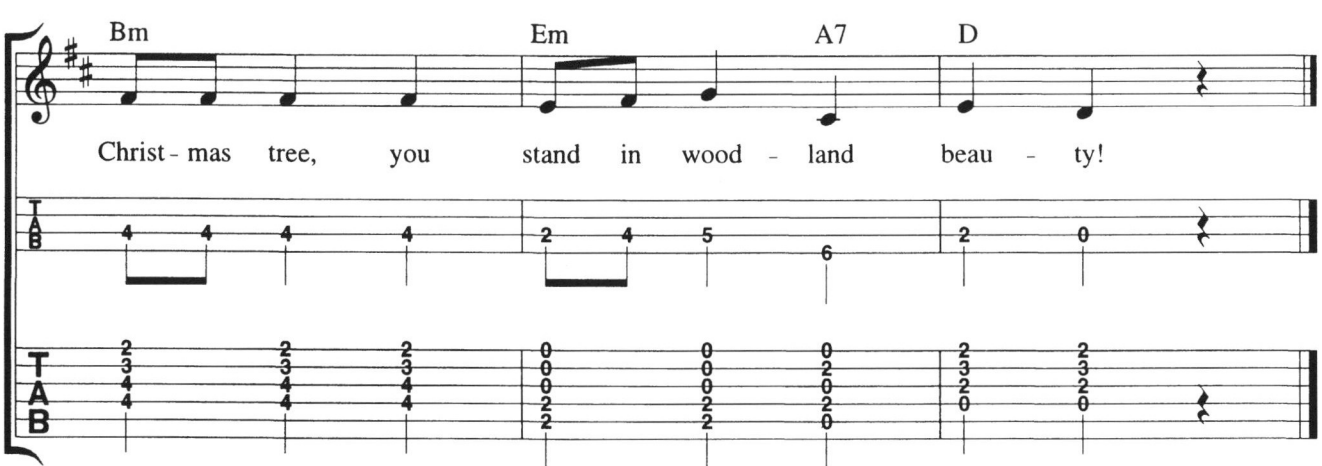

O CHRISTMAS TREE

Arr. by Steve Kaufman

1. O Christmas tree, O Christmas tree!
   Thou tree most fair and lovely!
   The sight of thee at Christmas tide
   Spreads hope and gladness far and wide.
   O Christmas tree, O Christmas tree!
   Thou tree most fair and lovely.

2. O Christmas tree, O Christmas tree!
   Thou hast a wondrous message:
   Thou dost proclaim the Savior's birth,
   Good will to men and peace on earth.
   O Christmas tree, O Christmas tree!
   Thou hast a wondrous message.

IT CAME UPON THE MIDNIGHT CLEAR

Arr. by Steve Kaufman

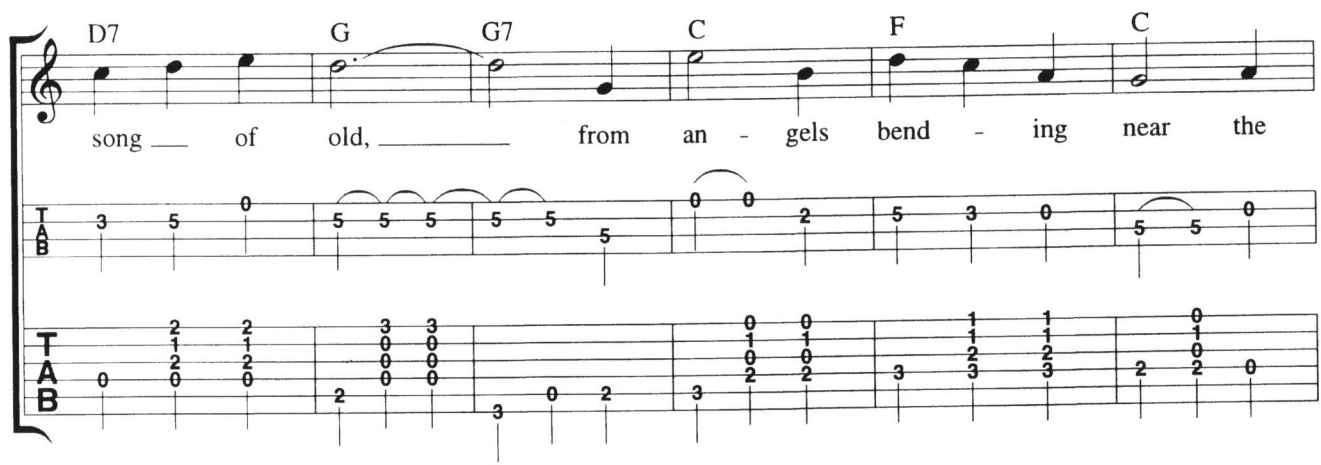

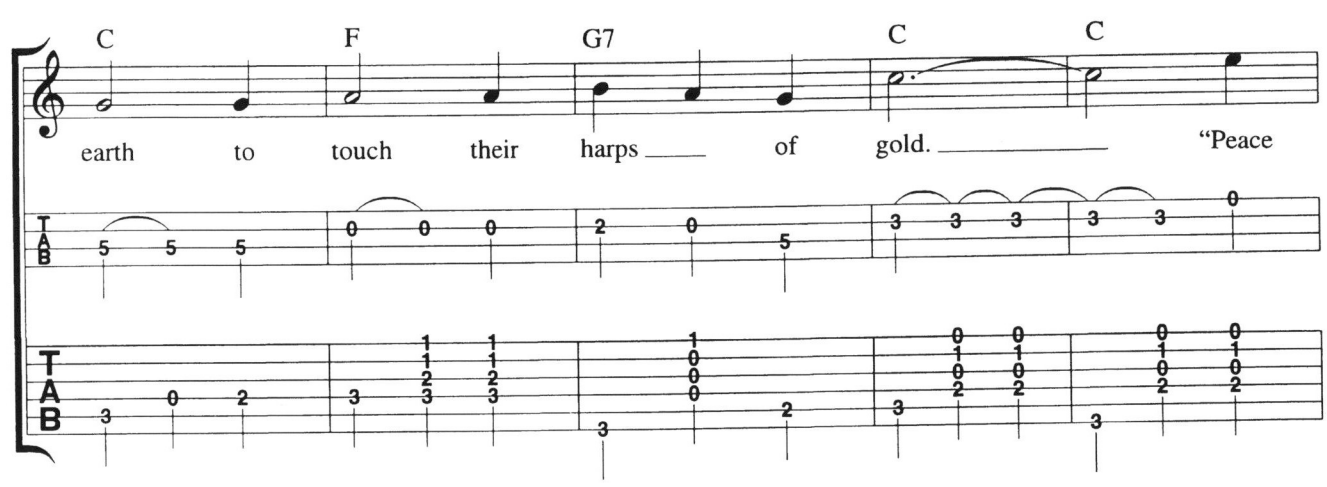

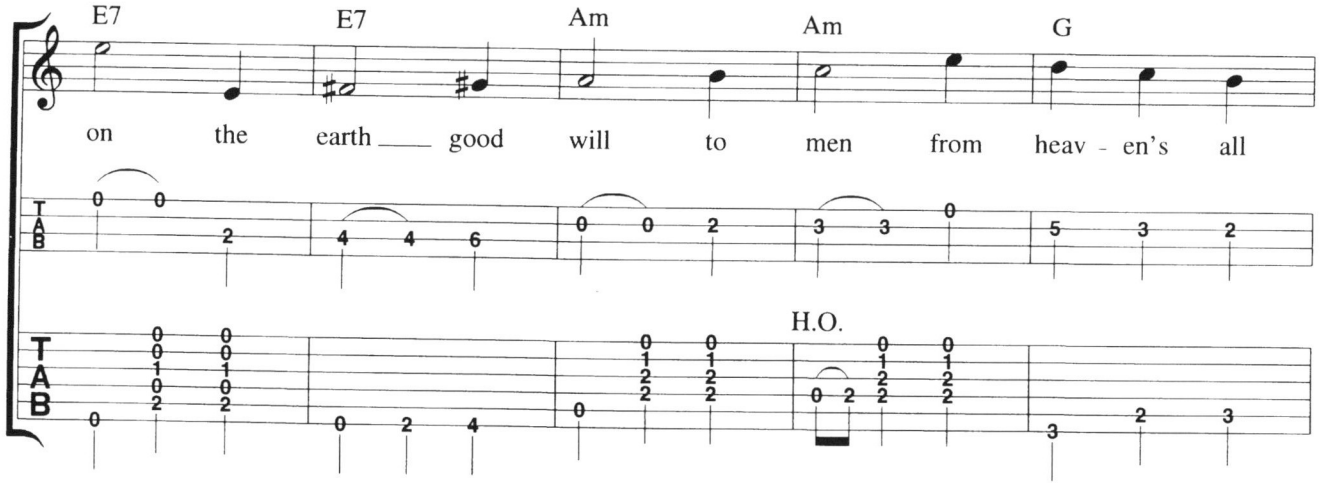

IT COME UPON THE MIDNIGHT CLEAR

Arr. by Steve Kaufman

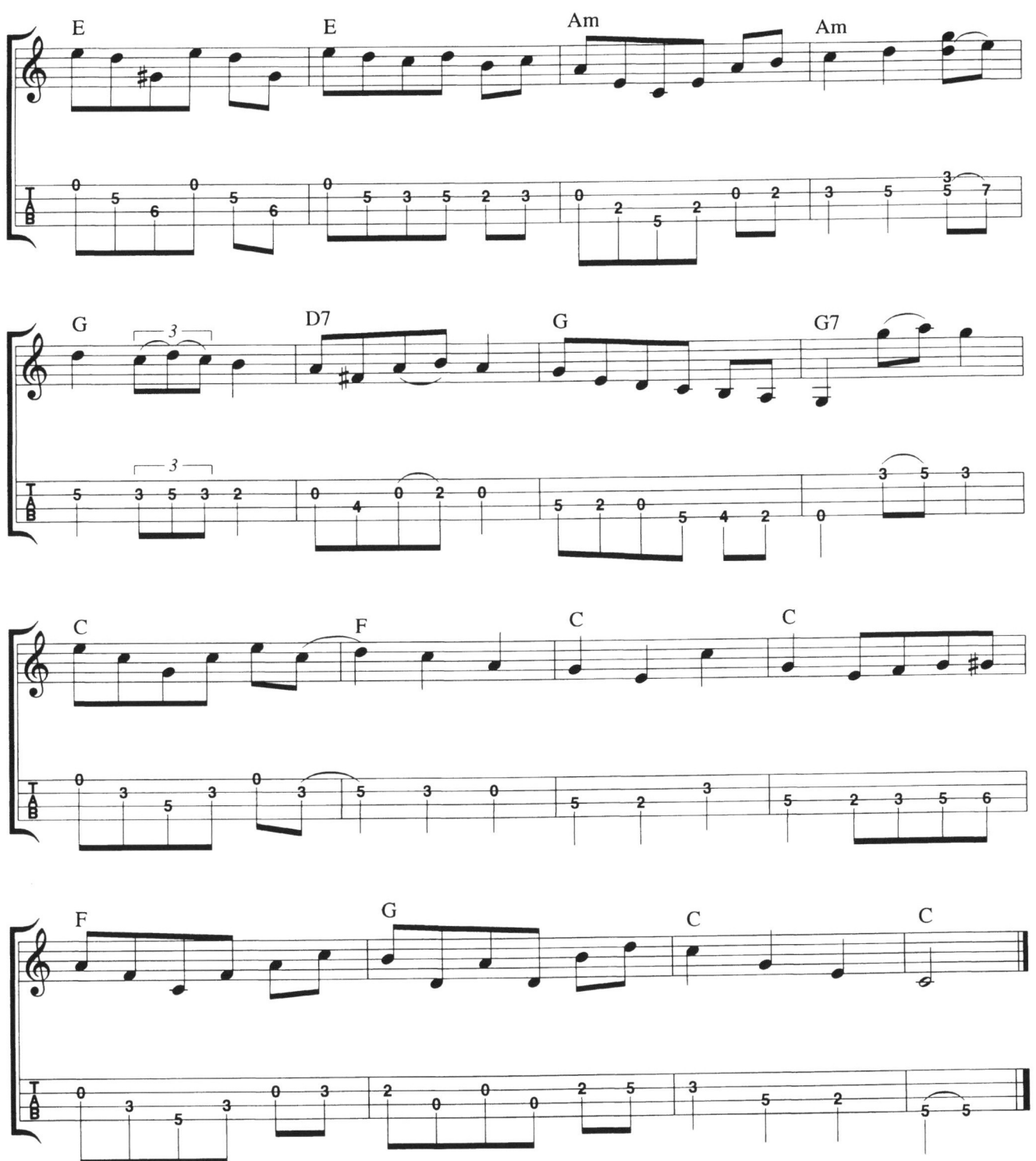

1. It came upon the midnight clear,
   That glorious song of old,
   From angels bending near the Earth,
   To touch their harps of gold:
   "Peace on Earth, good will to men,
   From heaven's all gracious King."
   The world in solemn stillness lay,
   To hear the angels sing.

2. Still through the cloven skies they come
   With peaceful wings unfurled,
   And still their heavenly music floats
   O'er all the weary world;
   Above its sad and lowly plains
   They bend on hovering wing,
   And ever o'er its Babel sound
   The blessed angels sing.

3. For lo! The days are hastening on,
   By prophet seen of old,
   When with the ever circling years
   Shall come the time foretold
   When peace shall over all the Earth
   Its ancient splendors fling,
   And the whole world send back the song
   Which now the angels sing. Amen.

GO TELL IT ON THE MOUNTAIN

Arr. by Steve Kaufman

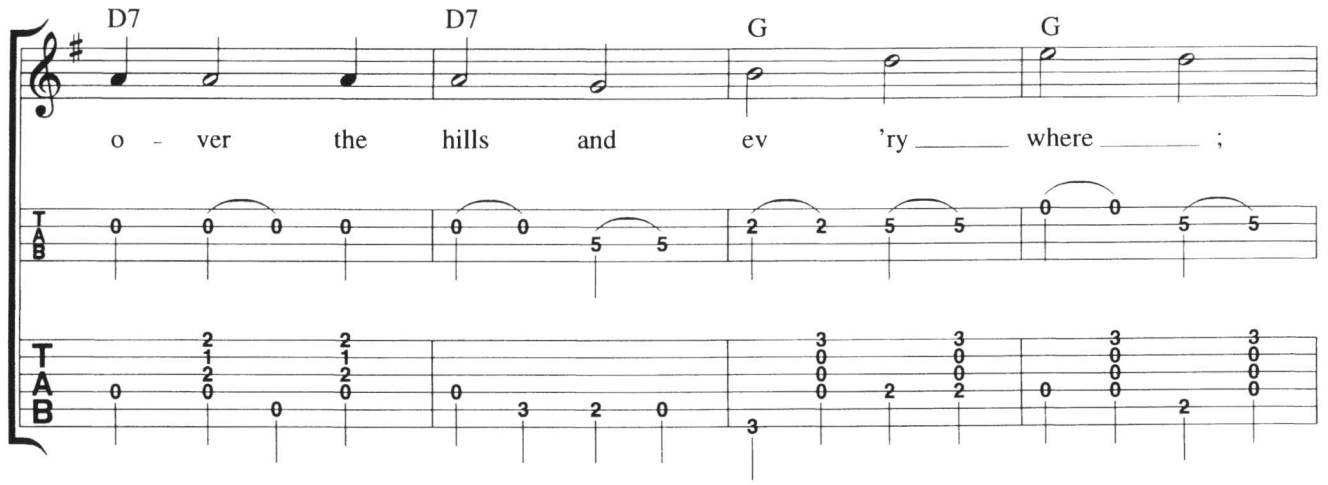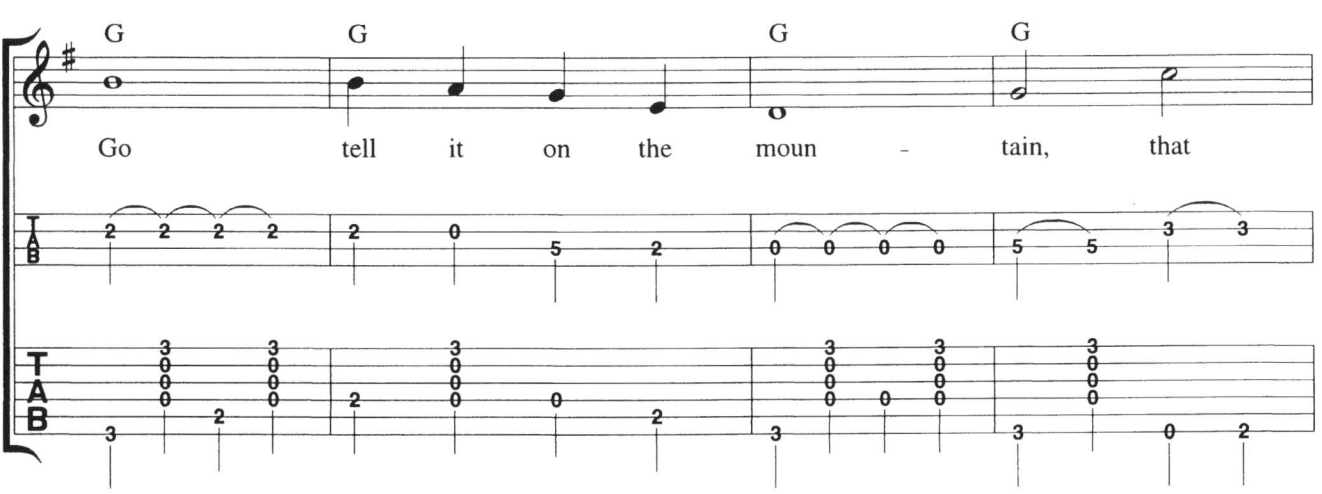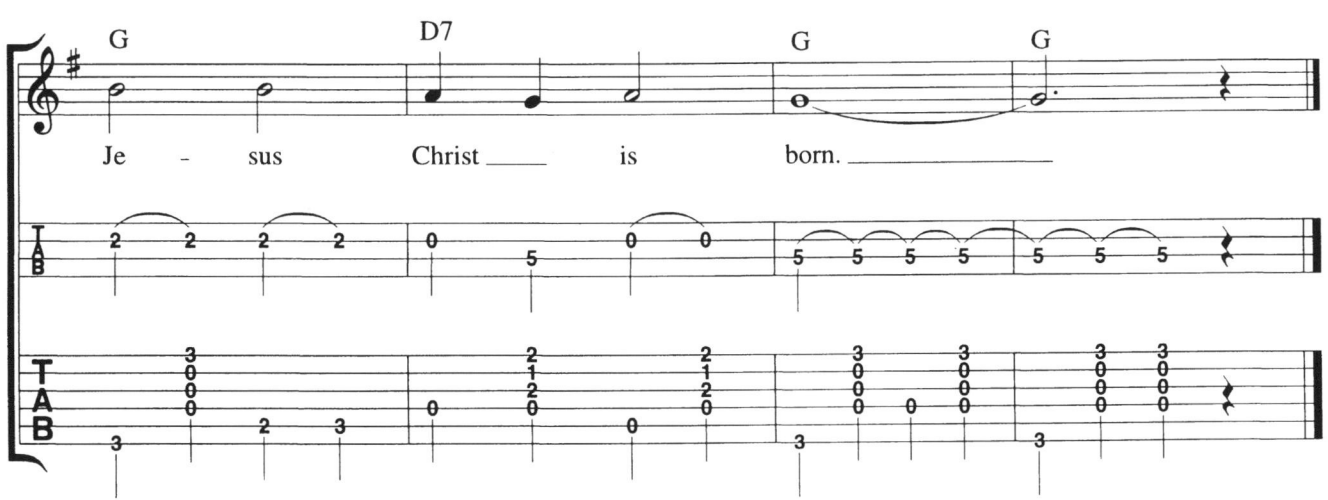

GO TELL IT ON THE MOUNTAIN

Arr. by Steve Kaufman

1. When I was a seeker,
   I sought both night and day,
   I sought the Lord to help me,
   And He showed me the way, Oh!

Chorus
  Go tell it on the mountain,
  Over the hills and everywhere,
  Go tell it on the mountain that
  Jesus Christ is born!

2. He made me a watchman
   Up on the city wall,
   And if I am a Christian,
   I am the least of all, Oh!
     Chorus

THE FIRST NOËL

Arr. by Steve Kaufman

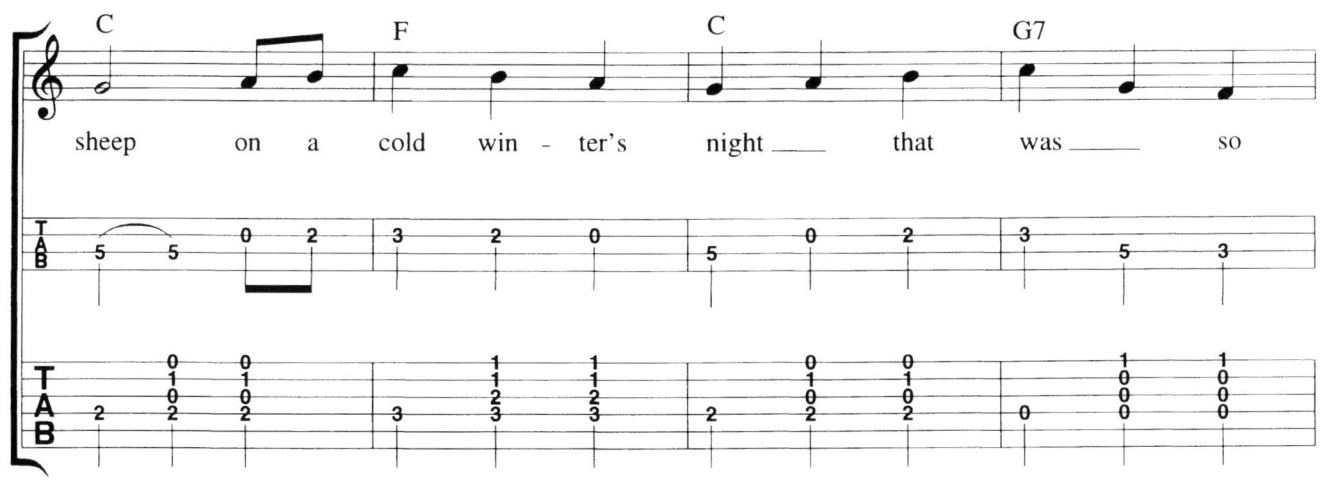
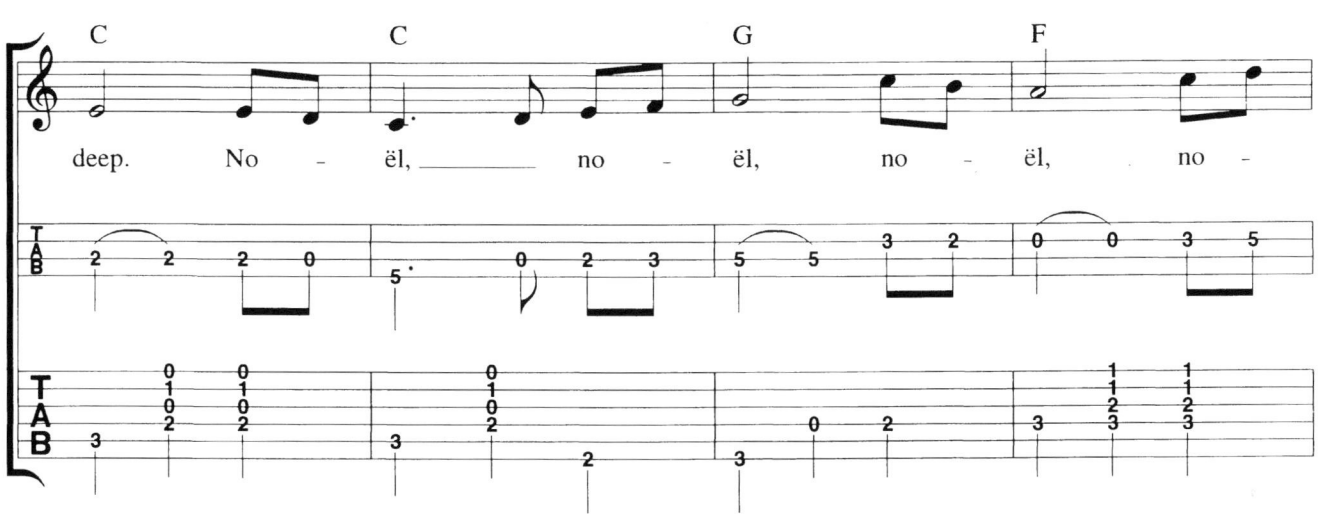
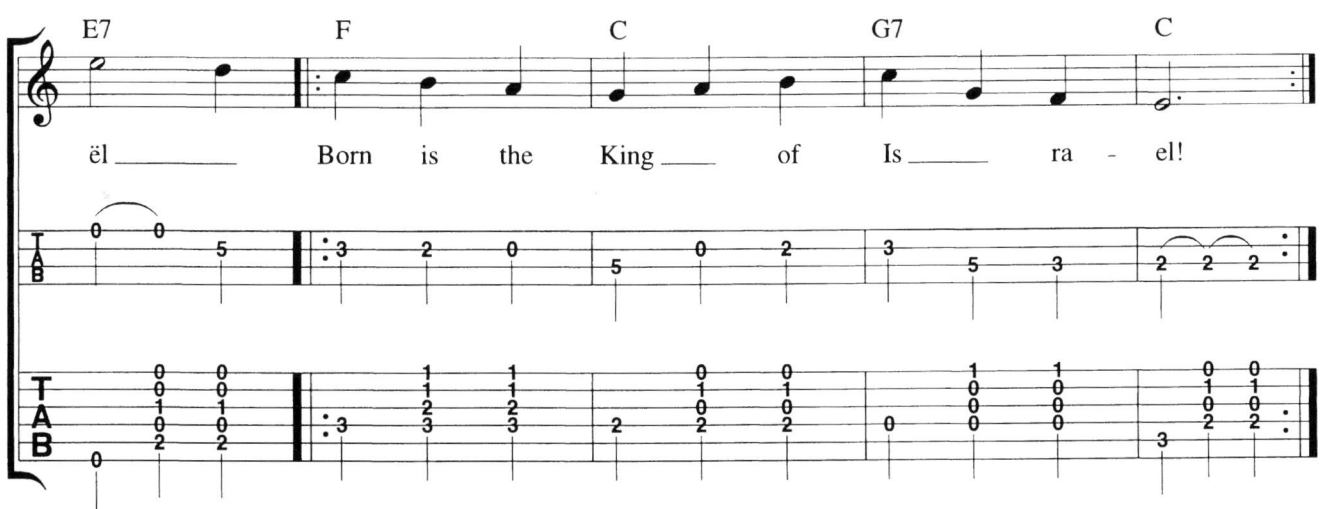

THE FIRST NOËL

Arr. by Steve Kaufman

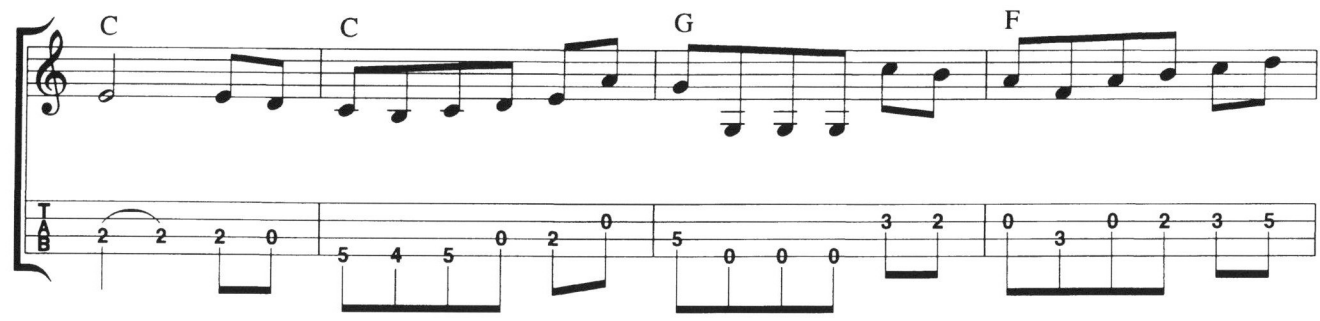
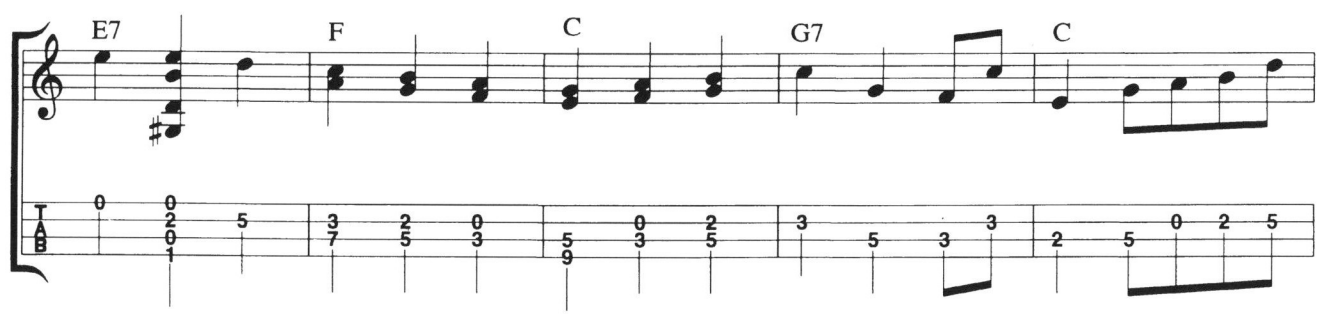
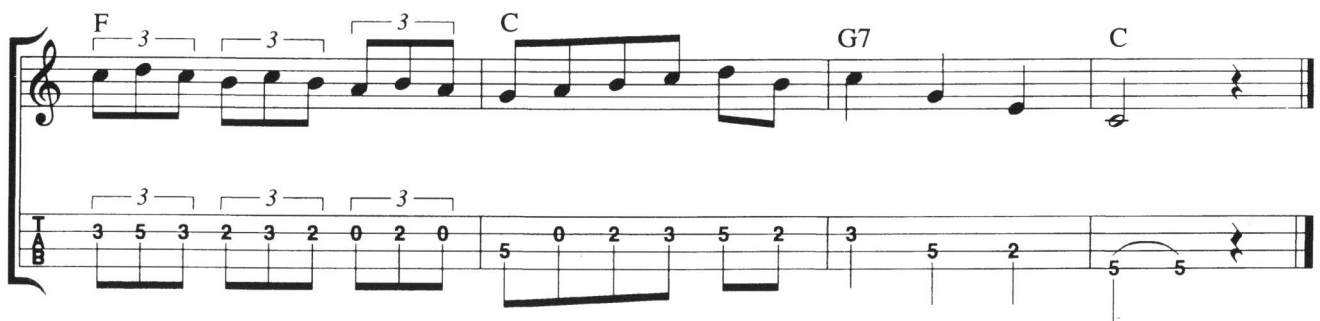

1. The first noël, the angels did say,
   Was to certain poor shepherds in fields as they lay,
   In the fields where they lay keeping their sheep
   On a cold winter's night that was so deep.

   Refrain
      Noël, Noël, Noël, Noël,
      Born is the King of Israel.

2. They looked up and saw a star
   Shining in the East, beyond them far,
   And to the Earth it gave great light,
   And so it continued both day and night.
         Refrain

3. And by the light of that same star
   Three wise men came from country far;
   To seek for a King was their intent,
   And to follow the star wherever it went.
         Refrain

4. This star drew nigh to the northwest;
   O'er Bethlehem it took its rest,
   And there it did both stop and stay,
   Right over the place where Jesus lay.
         Refrain

5. Then entered in those wise men three,
   Full reverently upon their knee,
   And offered there, in His presence
   Their gold and myrrh and frankincense.
         Refrain

WE THREE KINGS OF ORIENT ARE

John H. Hopkins   Arr. by Steve Kaufman

42

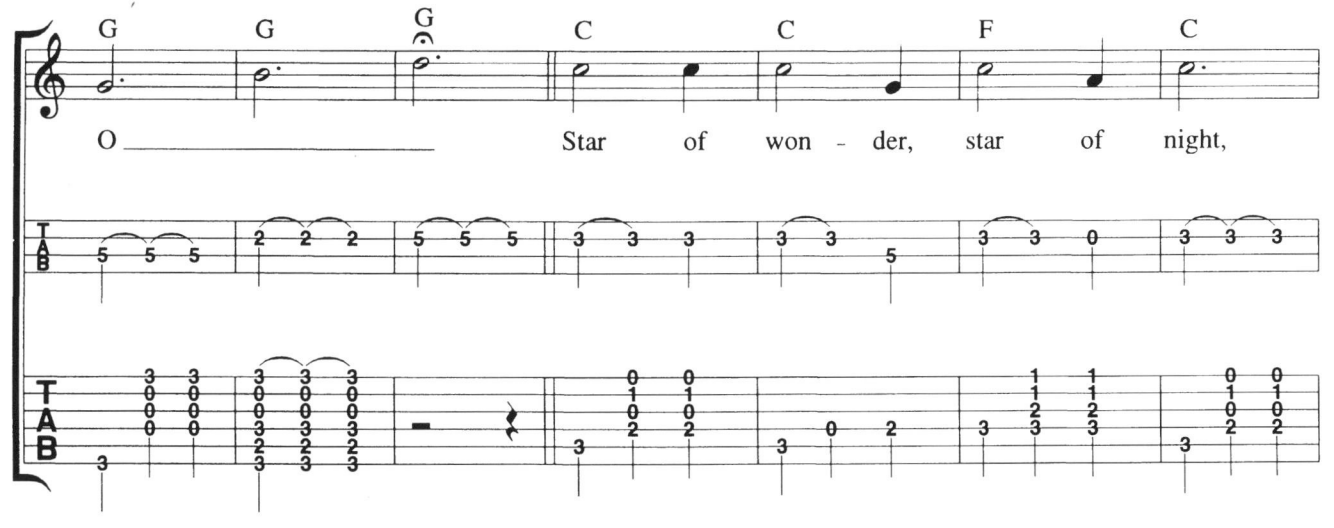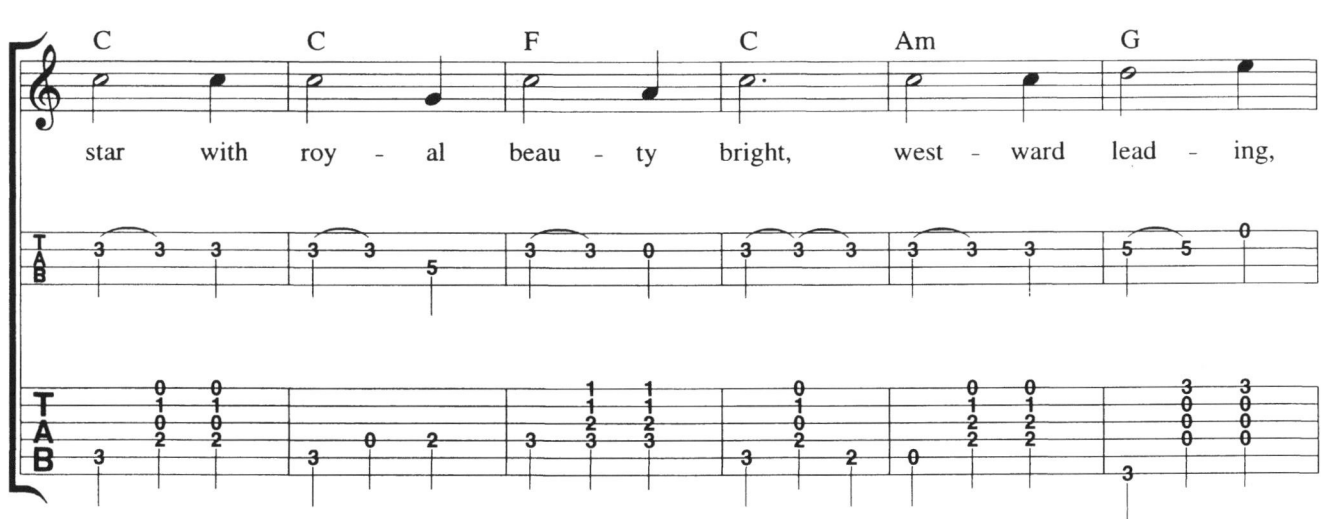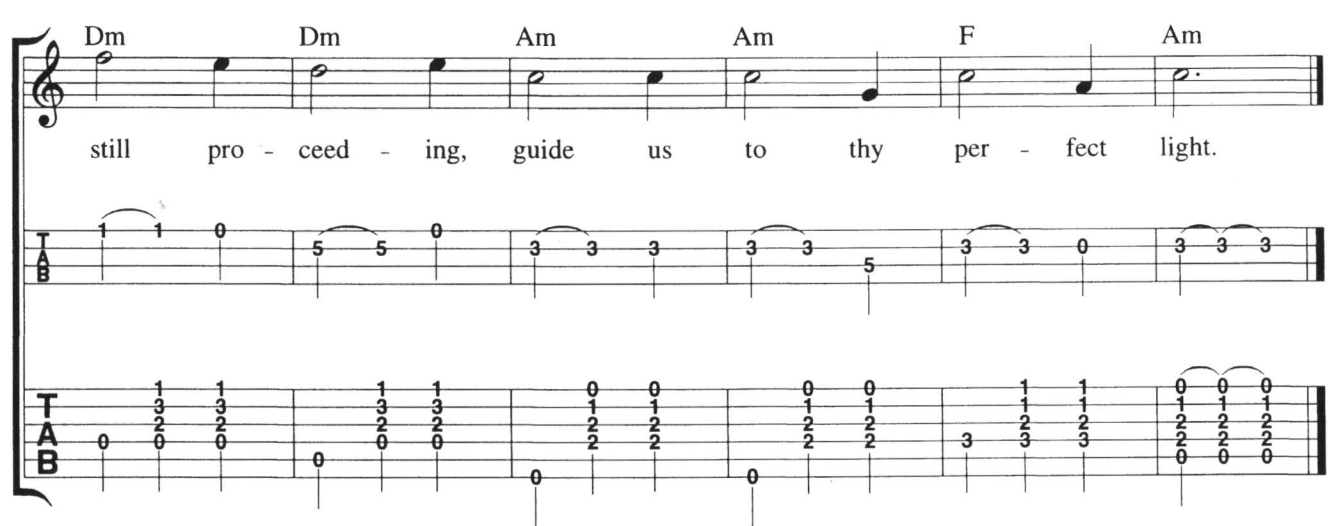

WE THREE KINGS OF ORIENT ARE

Arr. by Steve Kaufman

1. We three kings of Orient are;
   Bearing gifts we traverse afar,
   Field and fountain, moor and
     mountain,
   Following yonder star.

   Refrain
   O star of wonder, star of night,
   Star with royal beauty bright.
   Westward leading, still proceeding,
   Guide us to thy perfect light.

2. Born a King on Bethlehem's plain,
   Gold I bring to crown Him again,
   King forever, ceasing never
   Over us all to reign.
     Refrain

3. Frankincense to offer have I;
   Incense owns a Deity nigh;
   Prayer and praising all men raising,
   Worship Him, God on high.
     Refrain

4. Myrrh is mine: its bitter perfume
   Breathes a life of gathering gloom:
   Sorrowing, sighing, bleeding,
     dying,
   Sealed in the stone-cold tomb.
     Refrain

5. Glorious now behold Him arise,
   King and God and sacrifice;
   Alleluia, Alleluia!
   Sounds through the Earth and Skies.
     Refrain

O COME ALL YE FAITHFUL

TR. F. Oakeley, 1841

Arr. by Steve Kaufman
J.F. Wade, 1751

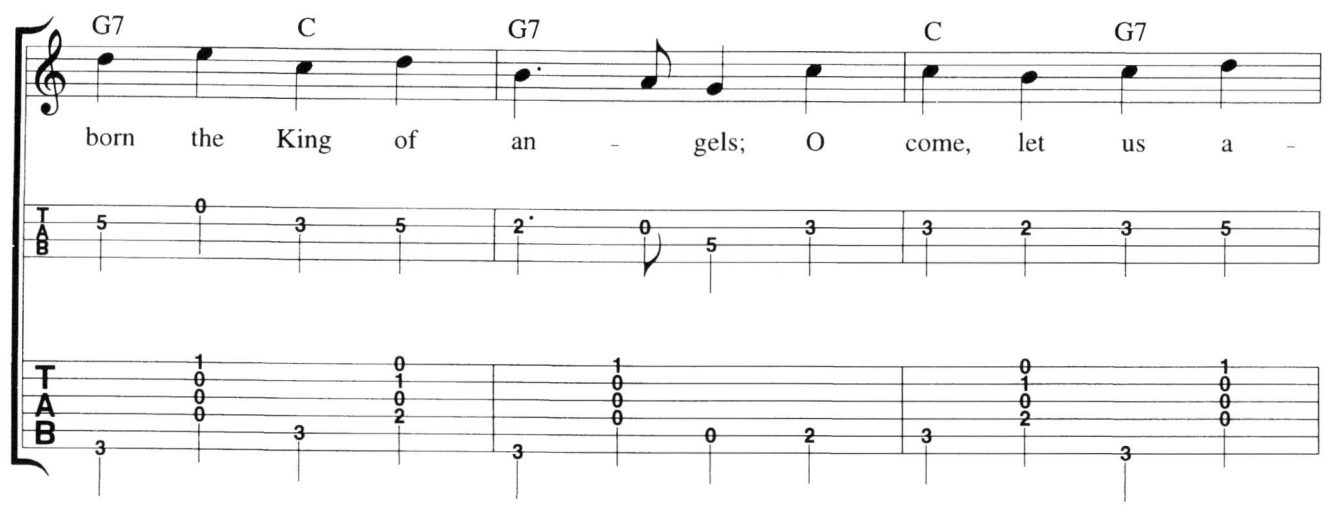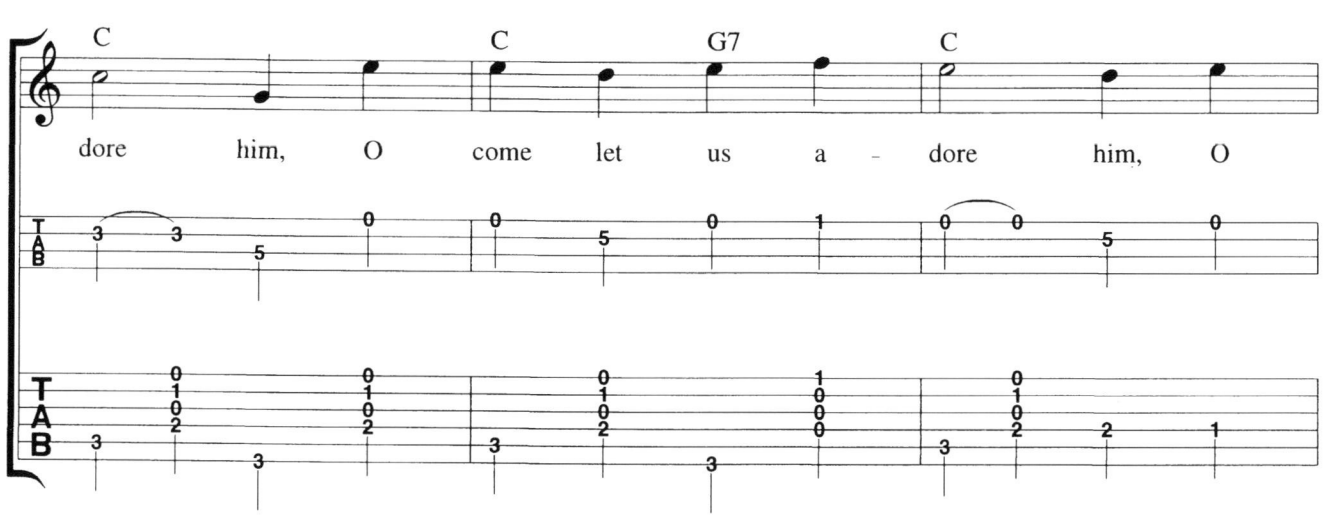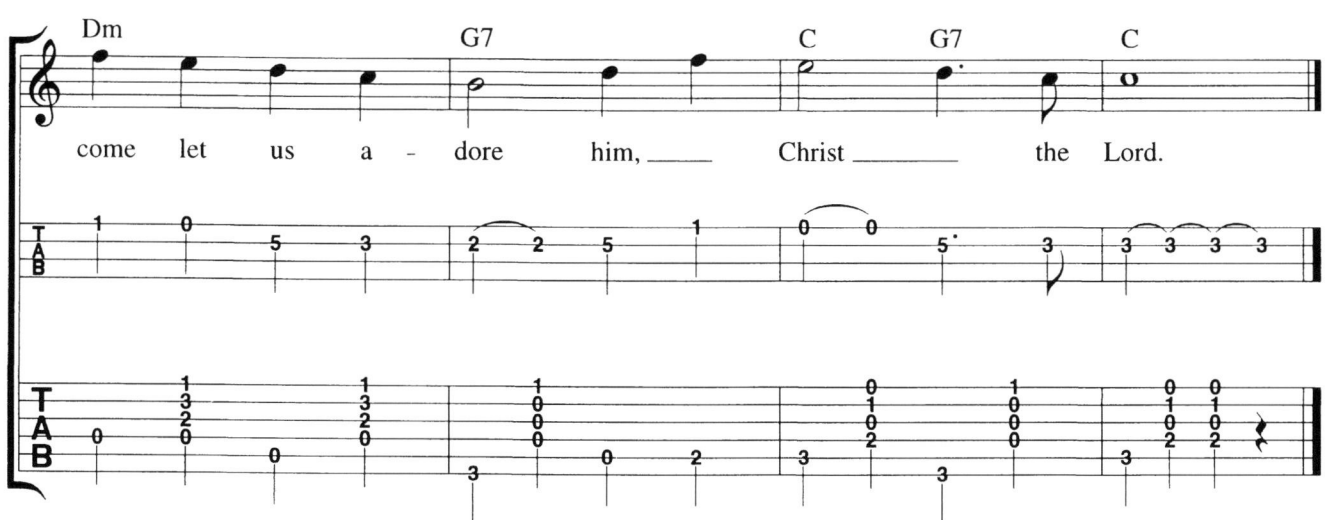

O COME ALL YE FAITHFUL

Arr. by Steve Kaufman

1. O come, all ye faithful,
   Joyful and triumphant,
   O come ye, O come ye to Bethlehem!
   Come and behold Him,
   Born the King of angels!
   O come, let us adore Him,
   O come, let us adore Him,
   O come, let us adore Him,
   Christ, the Lord!

2. Sing, choirs of angels,
   Sing in exultation,
   Sing, all ye citizens of heaven above!
   Glory to God,
   All glory in the highest!
   O come, let us adore Him,
   O come, let us adore Him,
   O come, let us adore Him,
   Christ, the Lord!

3. Yea, Lord, we greet thee,
   Born this happy morning,
   Jesus, to thee by all glory given;
   Word of the Father,
   Now in flesh appearing!
   O come, let us adore Him,
   O come, let us adore Him,
   O come, let us adore Him,
   Christ, the Lord!

   Amen

IN THE BLEAK MIDWINTER

Christina Rossetti

Arr. by Steve Kaufman
Gustau Holse

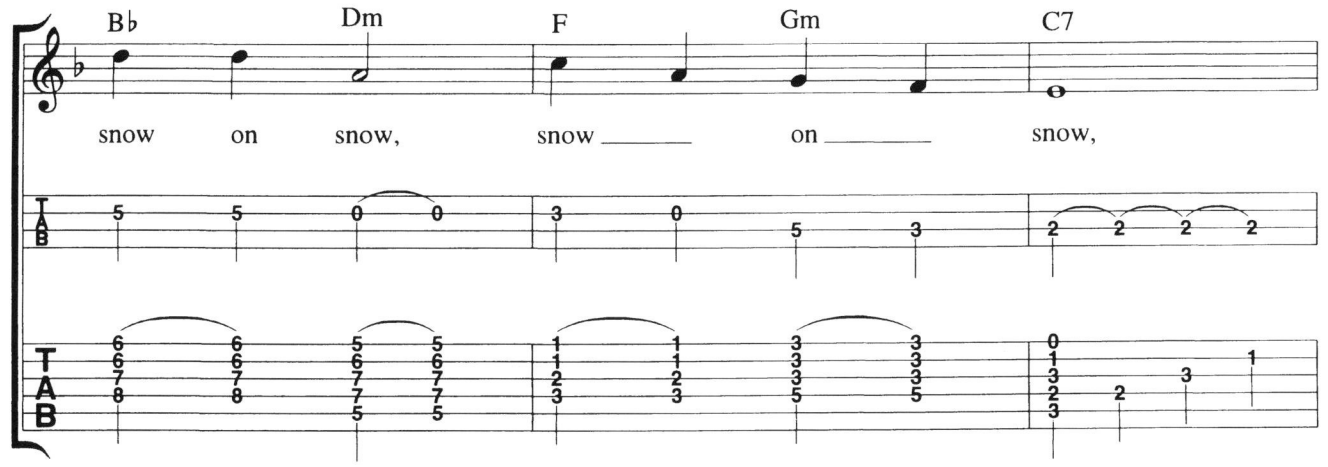

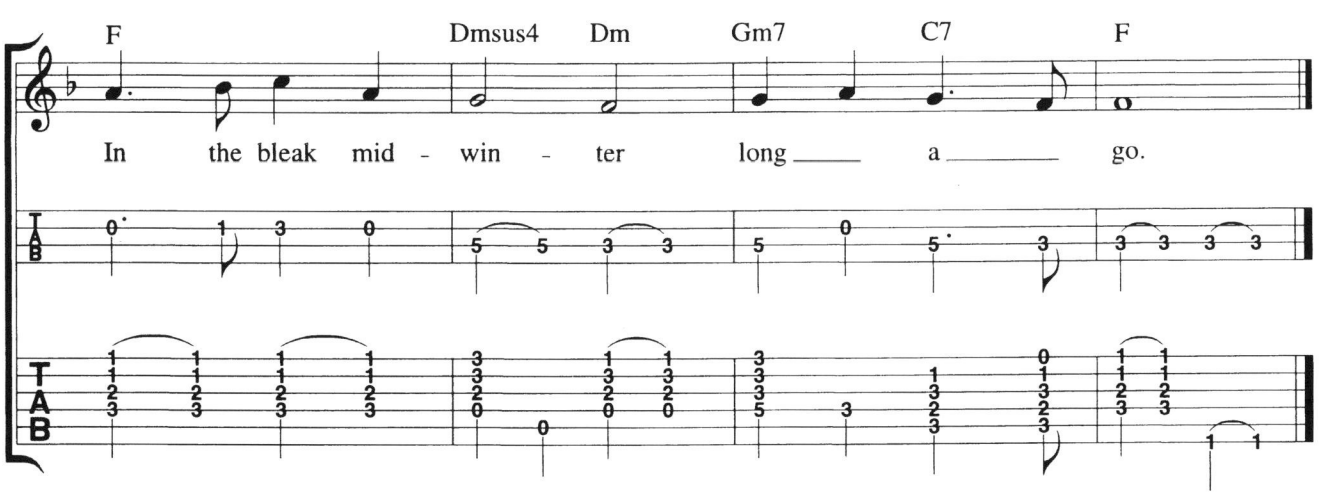

IN THE BLEAK MIDWINTER

Arr. by Steve Kaufman

1. In the bleak midwinter
   Frosty wind made moan,
   Earth stood hard as iron,
   Water like a stone;
   Snow had fallen, snow on snow,
   Snow on snow,
   In the bleak midwinter,
   Long ago.

2. Our God, heav'n cannot hold him
   Nor earth sustain;
   Heav'n and earth shall flee away
   When he comes to reign:
   In the bleak midwinter
   A stable place suffices
   The Lord God Almighty
   Jesus Christ.

3. Enough for him, whom cherubim
   Worship night and day,
   A breast full of milk,
   And a manger full of hay;
   Enough for him, whom angels
   Fall down before,
   The ox and ass and camel
   Which adore.

4. Angels and archangels
   May have gathered there,
   Cherubim and seraphim
   Thronged the air;
   But only his mother
   In her maiden bliss
   Worshipped the beloved
   With a kiss.

5. What can I give him,
   Poor as I am?
   If I were a shepherd
   I would bring a lamb;
   If I were a wise man
   I would do my part;
   Yet what I can give him,

BRING A TORCH, JEANETTE, ISABELLA

Arr. by Steve Kaufman

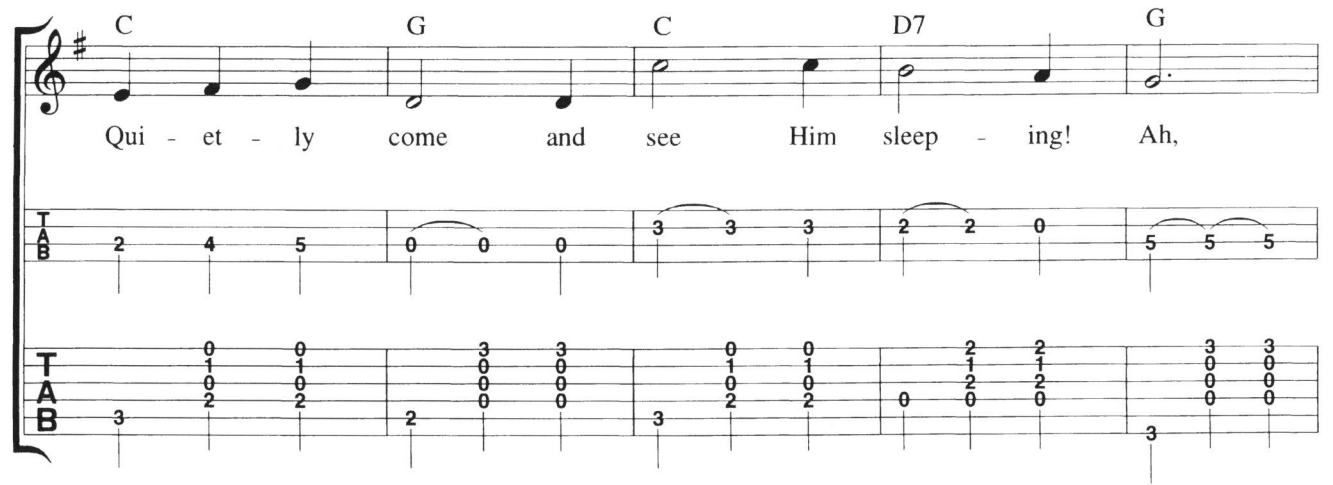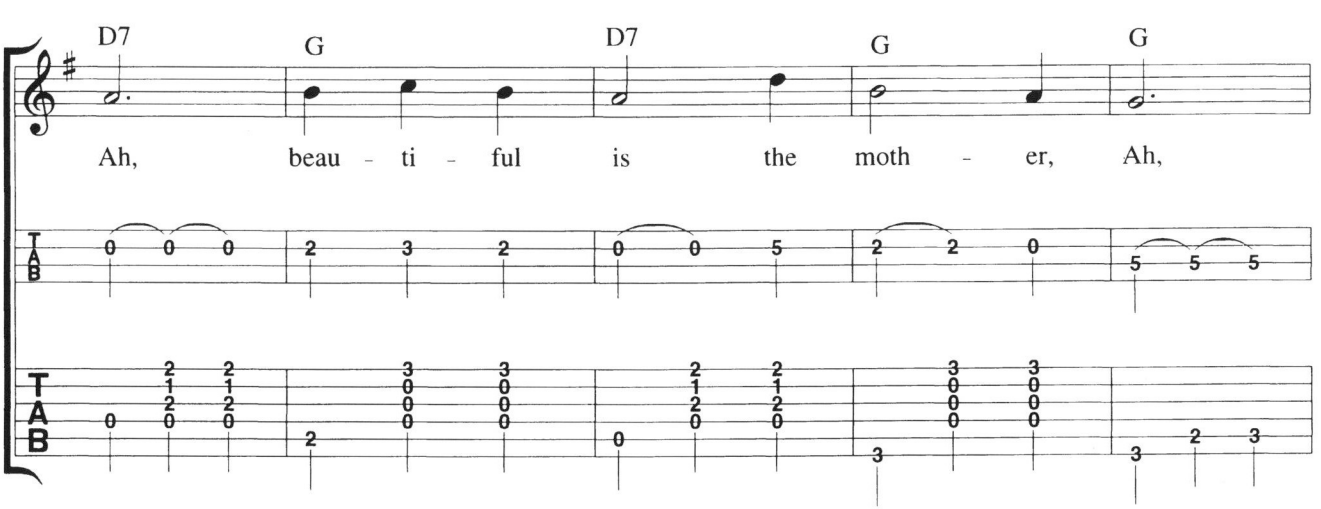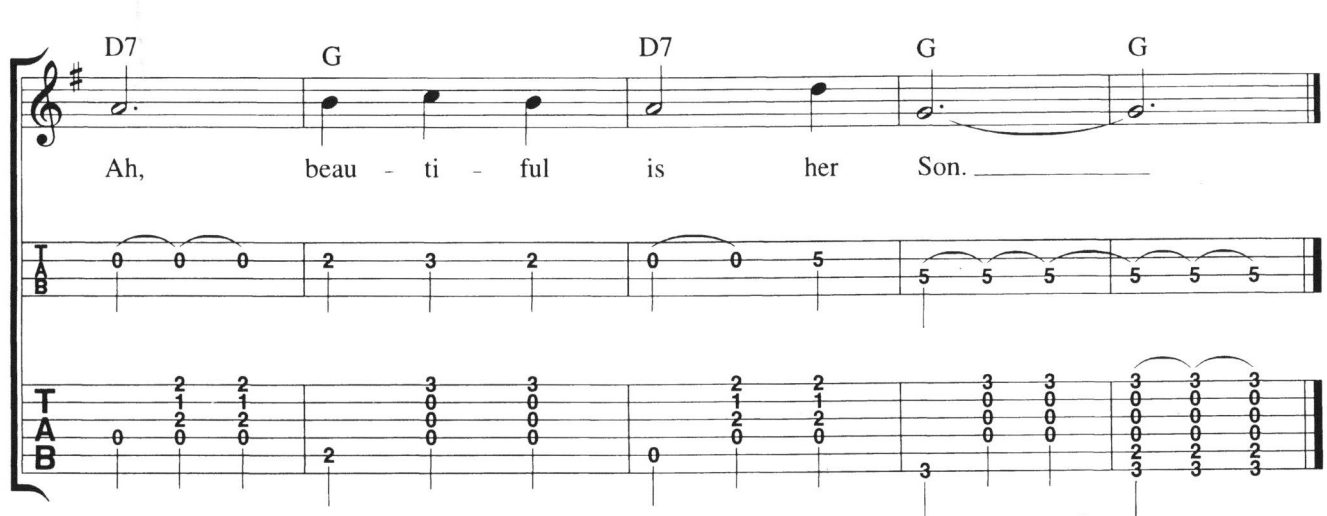

BRING A TORCH, JEANETTE, ISABELLA

Arr. by Steve Kaufman

56

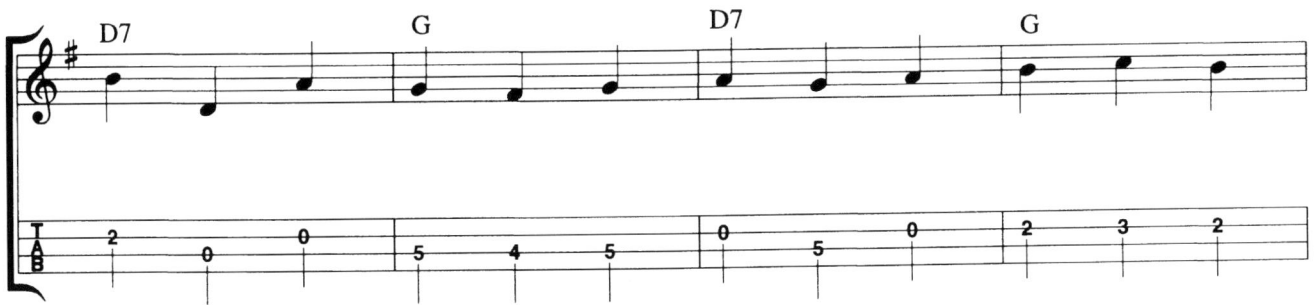

1. Bring a torch, Jeannette, Isabella!
   Bring a torch to the cradle run!
   It is Jesus, good folk of the
     village;
   Christ is born and Mary's calling:
   Ah! Ah! Beautiful is the Mother!
   Ah! Ah! Beautiful is her Son!

2. It is wrong when the child is sleeping,
   It is wrong to talk so loud;
   Silence, all, as you gather around Him,
   Lest your noise shall Jesus;
   Hush! Hush! See how fast He
     slumbers,
   Hush! Hush! See how fast He sleeps!

3. Softly to the little stable,
   Softly for a moment to come;
   Look and see how charming is Jesus,
   How He is white, His cheeks are rosy!
   Hush! Hush! See how the Child is
     sleeping;
   Hush! Hush! See how He smiles and dreams.

AWAY IN A MANGER

Martin Luther, 1483–1546

Arr. by Steve Kaufman

58

AWAY IN A MANGER

Arr. by Steve Kaufman

1. Away in a manger, no crib for His bed
   The little Lord Jesus laid down His sweet head
   The stars in the sky looked down where He lay,
   The little Lord Jesus, asleep on the hay.

2. The cattle are lowing, the Baby awakes,
   But little Lord Jesus, no crying He makes.
   I love Thee, Lord Jesus, look down from the sky,
   And stay by my cradle till morning is nigh.

3. Be near me, Lord Jesus, I ask Thee to stay
   Close by me forever, and love me, I pray.
   Bless all the dear children in thy tender care,
   And fit us for heaven to live with Thee there.

ANGELS WE HAVE HEARD ON HIGH

The Westminster Carol

Arr. by Steve Kaufman

62

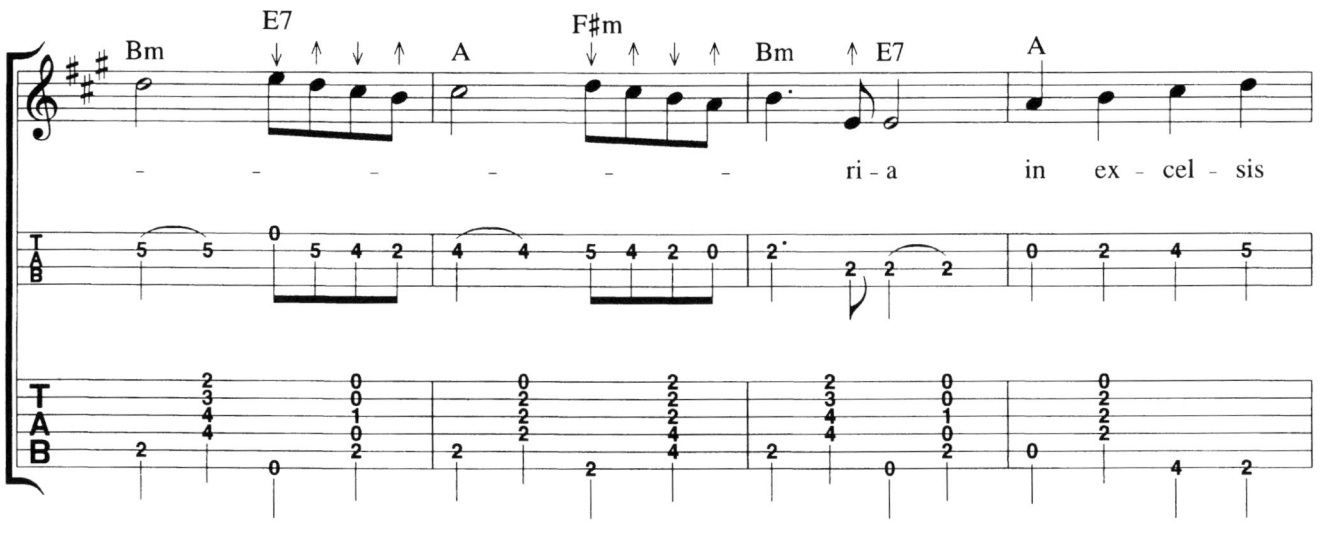
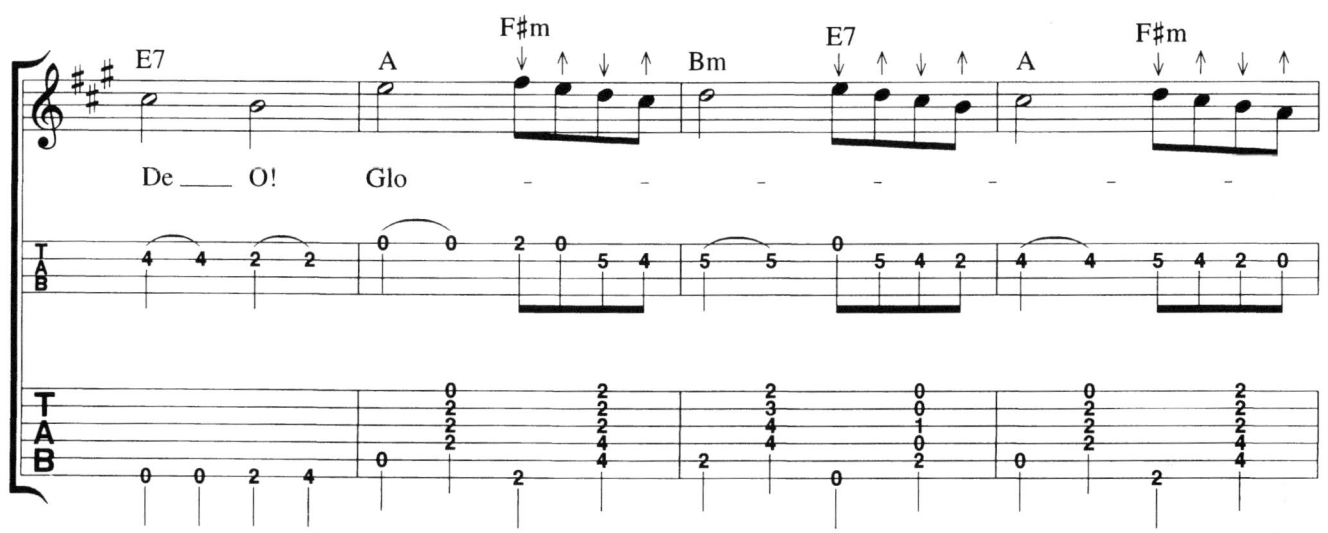
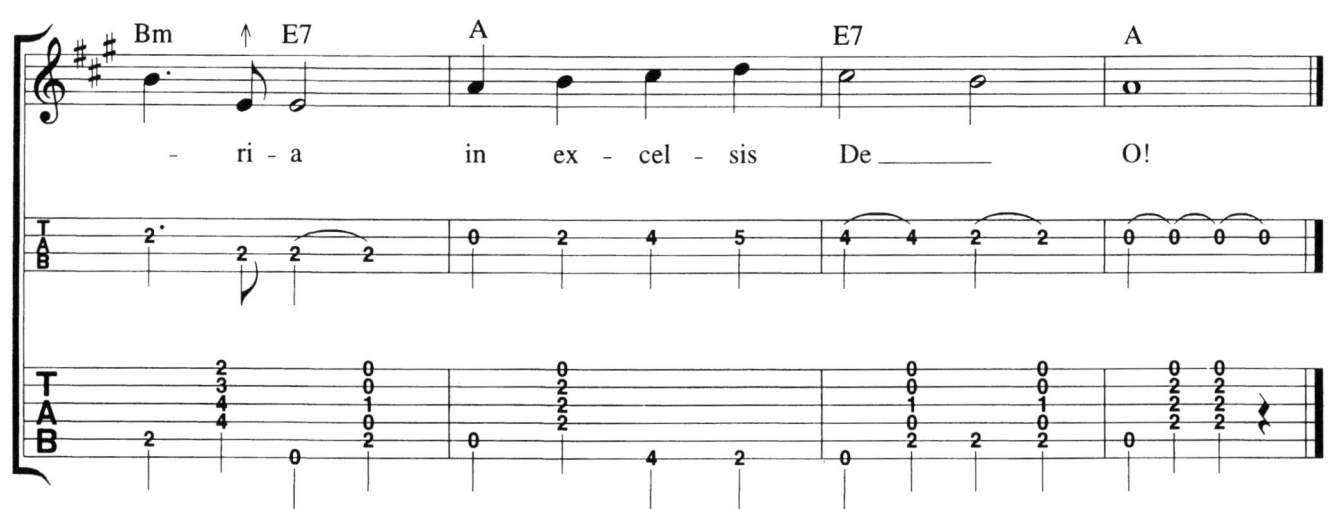

63

ANGELS WE HAVE HEARD ON HIGH

Arr. by Steve Kaufman

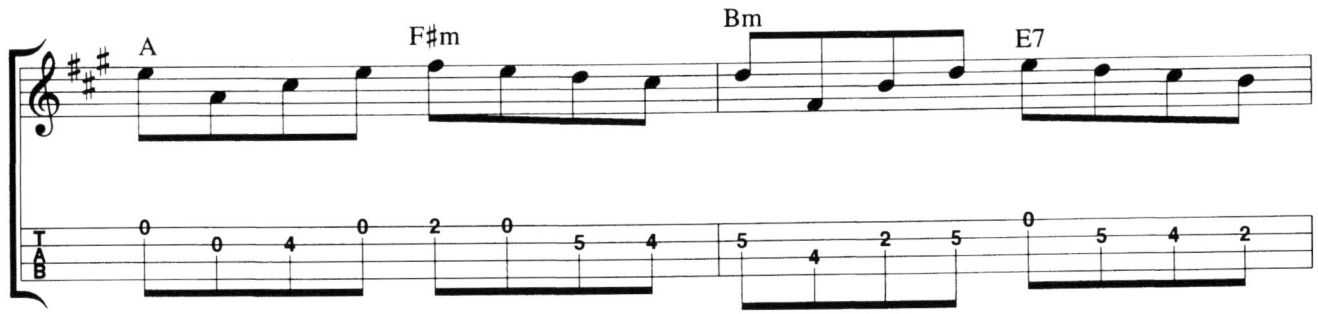
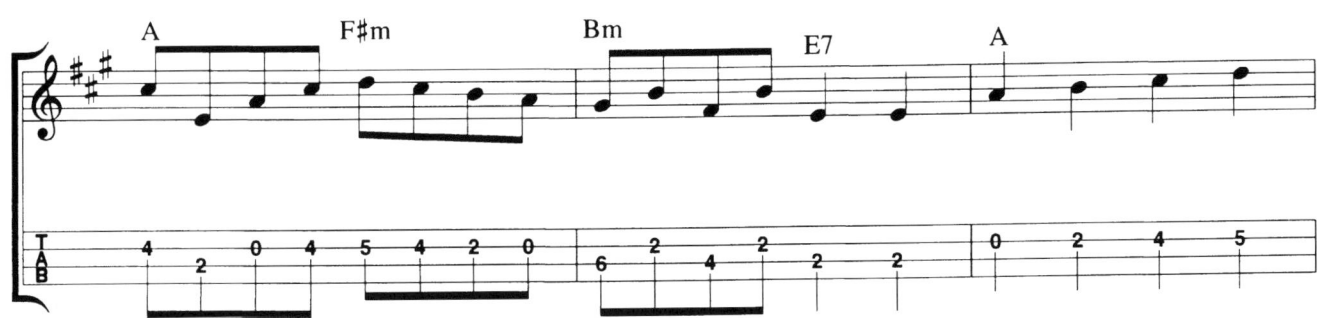

1. Angels we have heard on high,
   Sweetly singing o'er the plains;
   And the mountains in reply,
   Echoing their joyous strains.

   Refrain
       Gloria in excelsis Deo,
       Gloria in excelsis Deo.

2. Shepherds, why this jubilee?
   Why your joyous strains prolong?
   What the gladsome tidings be
   Which inspire your heavenly song?
       Refrain

3. Come to Bethlehem, and see
   Him whose birth the angels sing;
   Come, adore on bended knee
   Christ the Lord, the newborn King.
       Refrain

4. See him in a manger laid,
   Whom the choirs of angels praise;
   Mary, Joseph, lend your aid,
   While the hearts in love we raise.
       Refrain

WHAT CHILD IS THIS?

Arr. by Steve Kaufman

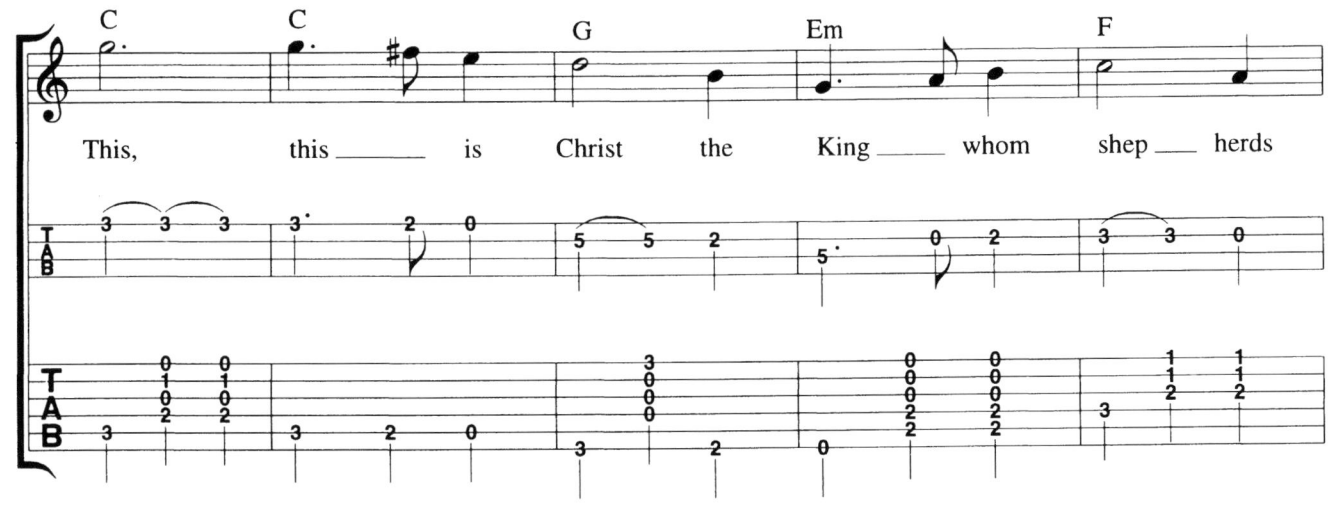
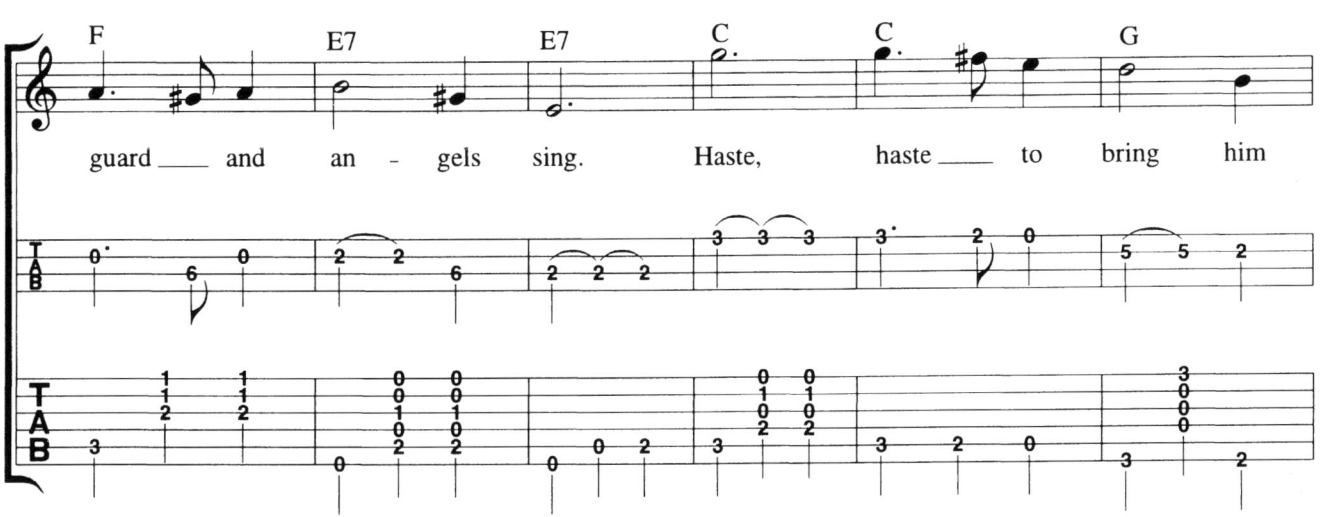
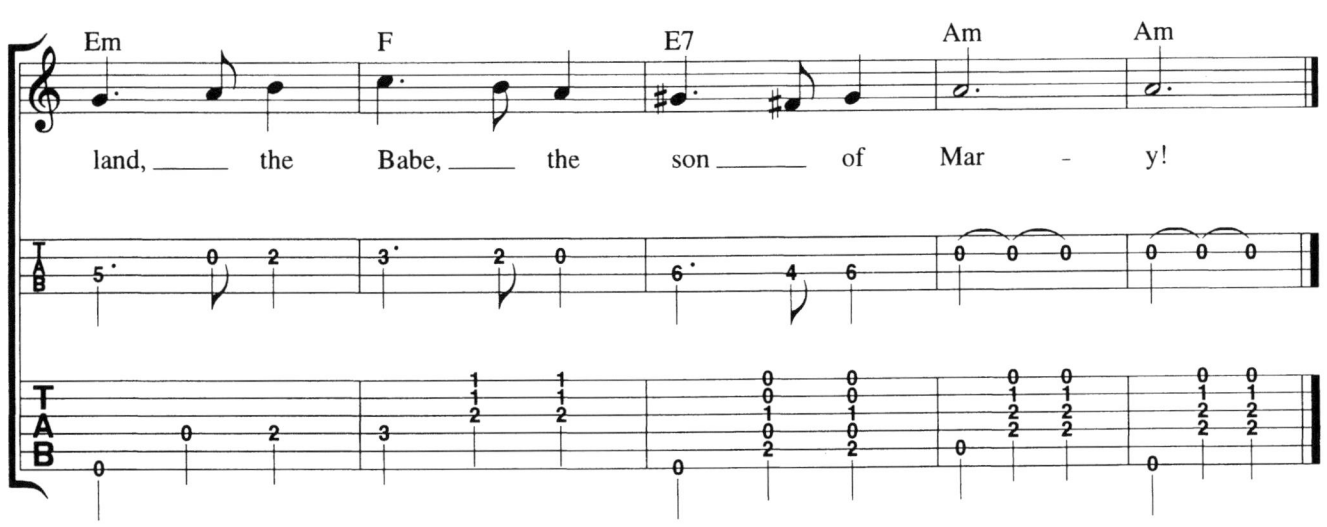

67

WHAT CHILD IS THIS?

Arr. by Steve Kaufman

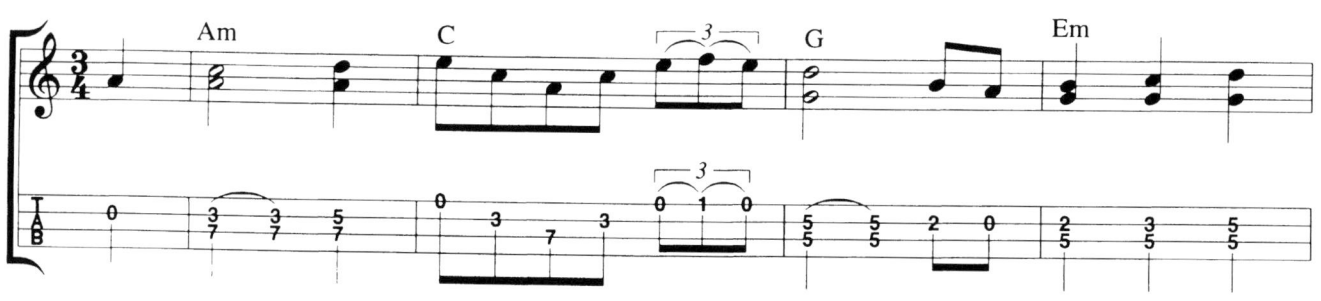

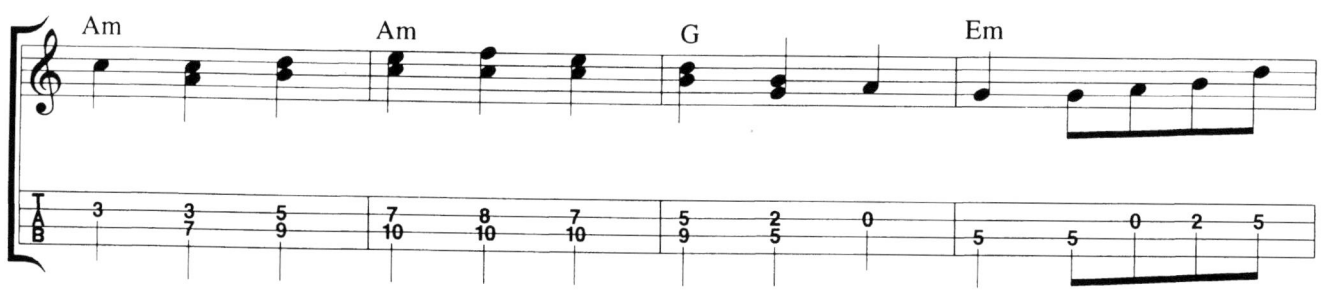
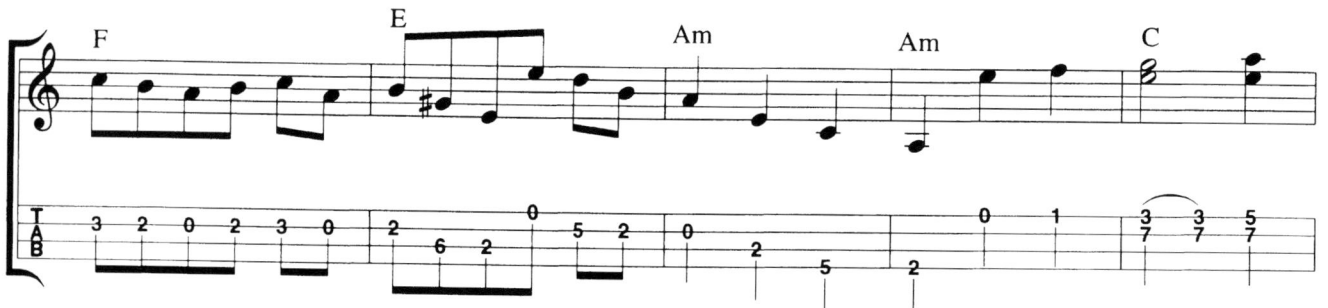

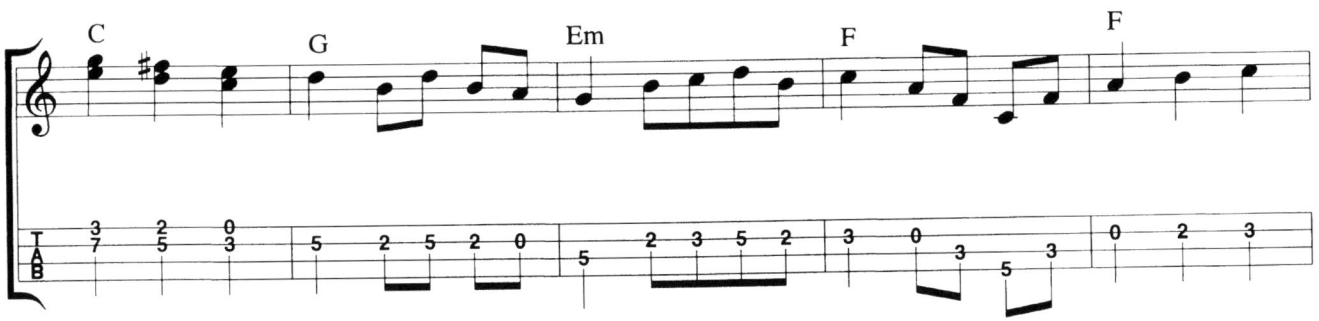

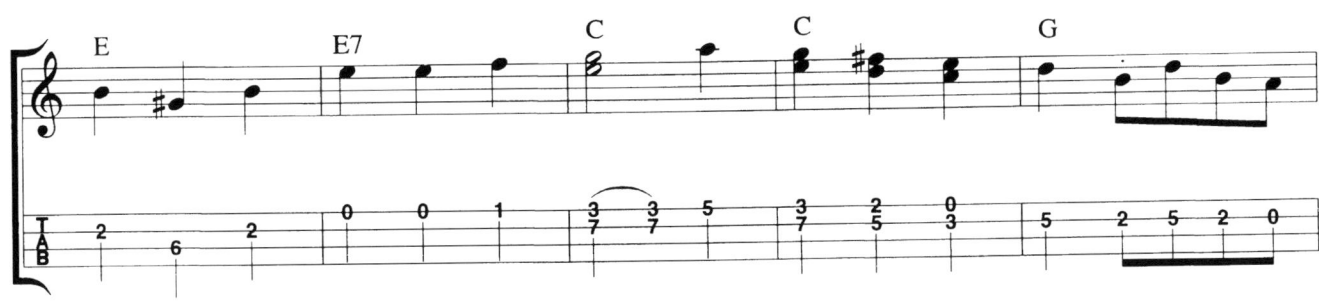

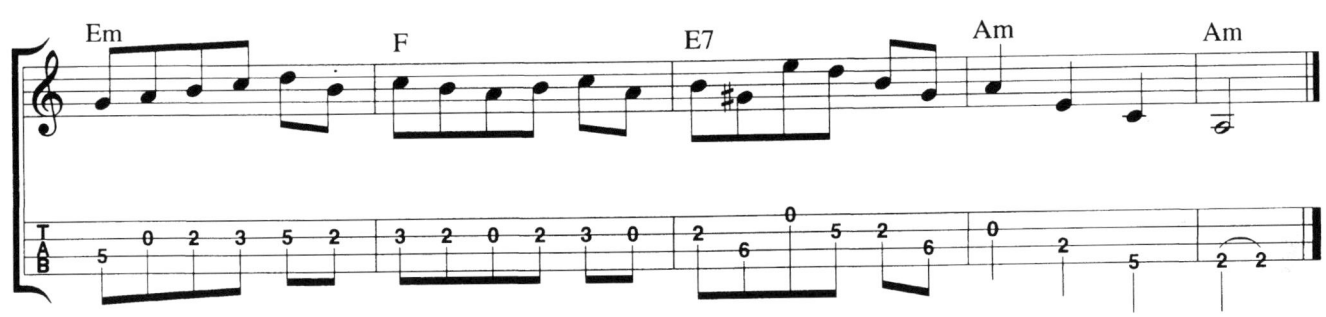

1. What child is this who, laid to rest,
   On Mary's lap is sleeping?
   Whom angels greet with anthems sweet,
   While shepherds watch are keeping?

   Refrain
     This, this is Christ the King,
     Whom shepherds guard and angels sing:
     Haste, haste to bring him laud,
     The babe, the Son of Mary.

2. Why lies he in such mean estate
   Where ox and ass are feeding?
   Good Christian, fear: For sinners here
   The silent Word is pleading.
       Refrain

3. So bring him incense, gold and myrrh;
   Come, peasant, King, to own him;
   The king of kings salvation brings.
   Let loving hearts enthrone him!
       Refrain

DECK THE HALLS

Arr. by Steve Kaufman

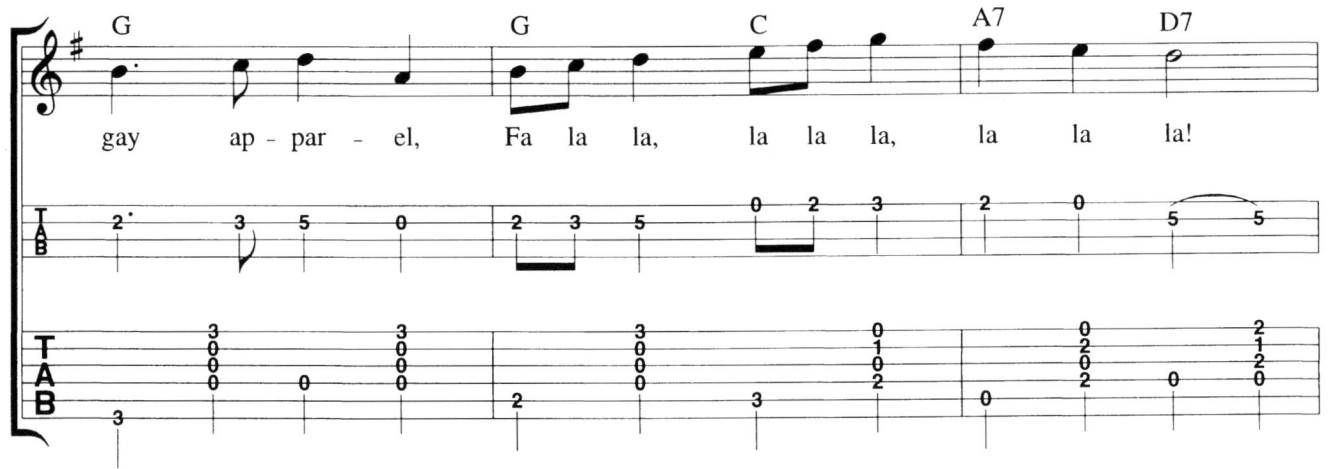
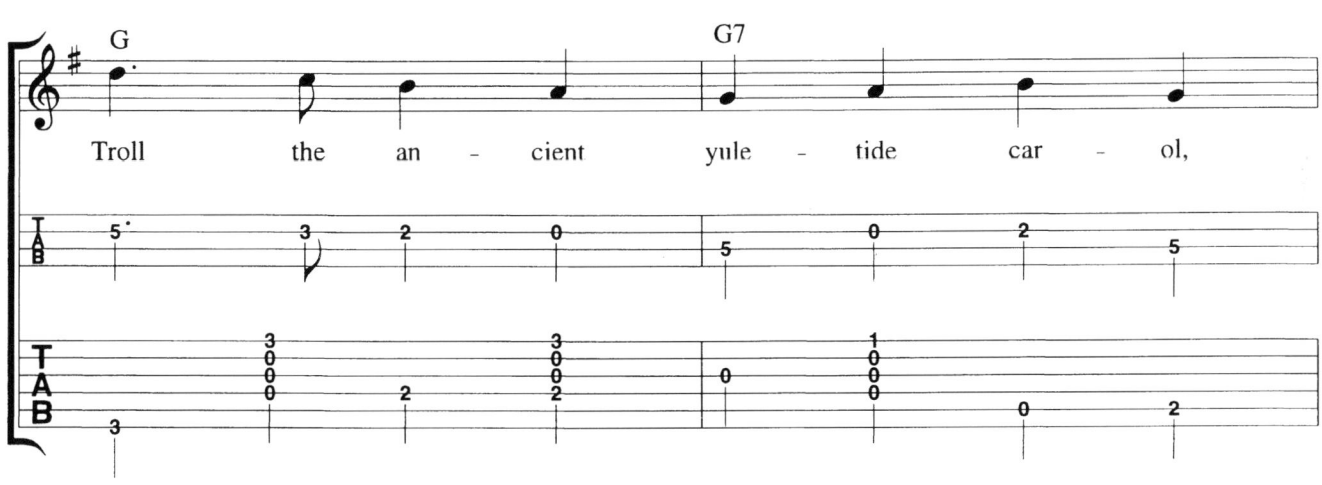
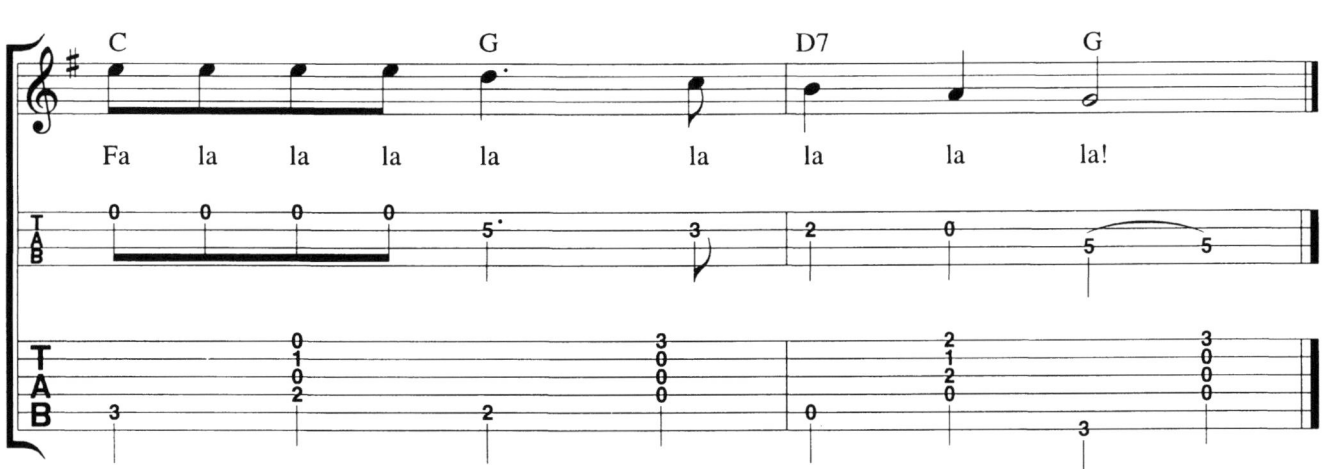

DECK THE HALLS

Arr. by Steve Kaufman

1. Deck the halls with boughs of holly,
   Fa la la la la, la la la la la
   "Tis the season to be jolly,
   Fa la la la la, la la la la la.
   Don we now our gay apparel,
   Fa la la, la la la la la,
   Troll the ancient Yuletide carol,
   Fa, la, la, la, la, la, la, la, la.

2. See the Blazing Yule before us,
   Fa la la la la, la la la la la
   Strike the harp and join the chorus,
   Fa la la la la, la la la la la.
   Follow me in merry measure,
   Fa la la, la la la la la,
   While I tell of Yuletide treasure
   Fa, la, la, la, la, la, la, la, la.

3. Fast away the old year passes,
   Fa la la la la, la la la la la.
   Hail the new, ye lads and lasses,
   Fa la la la la, la la la la la.
   Sing we joyous all together,
   Fa la la, la la la la la,
   Heedless of the wind and weather,

ONCE IN ROYAL DAVID'S CITY

Words by Cecil Frances Alexander

Arr. by Steve Kaufman
Tune by Henry J. Gaundett

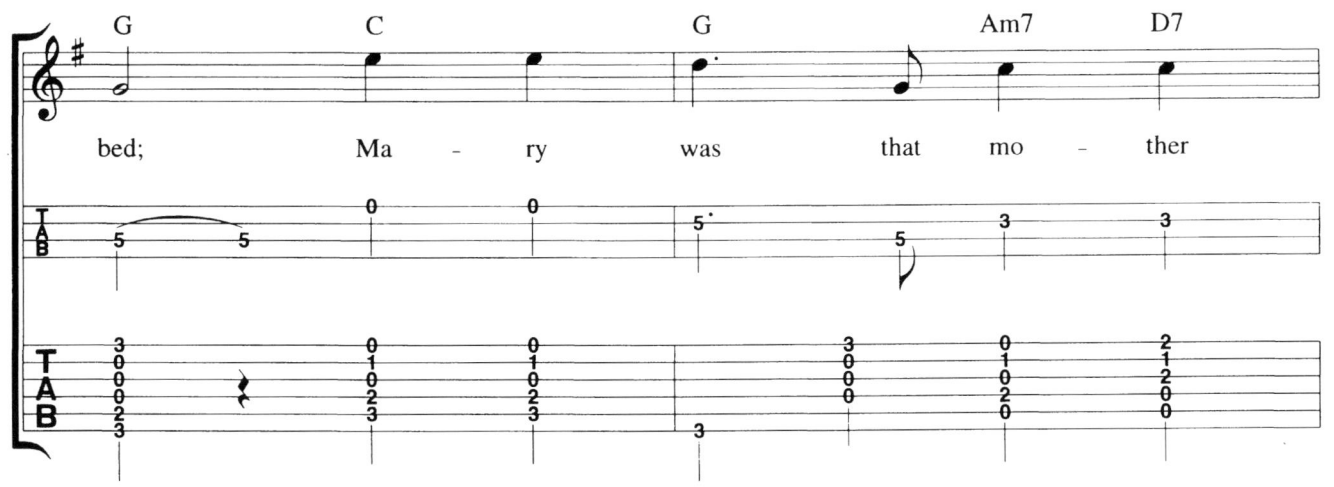
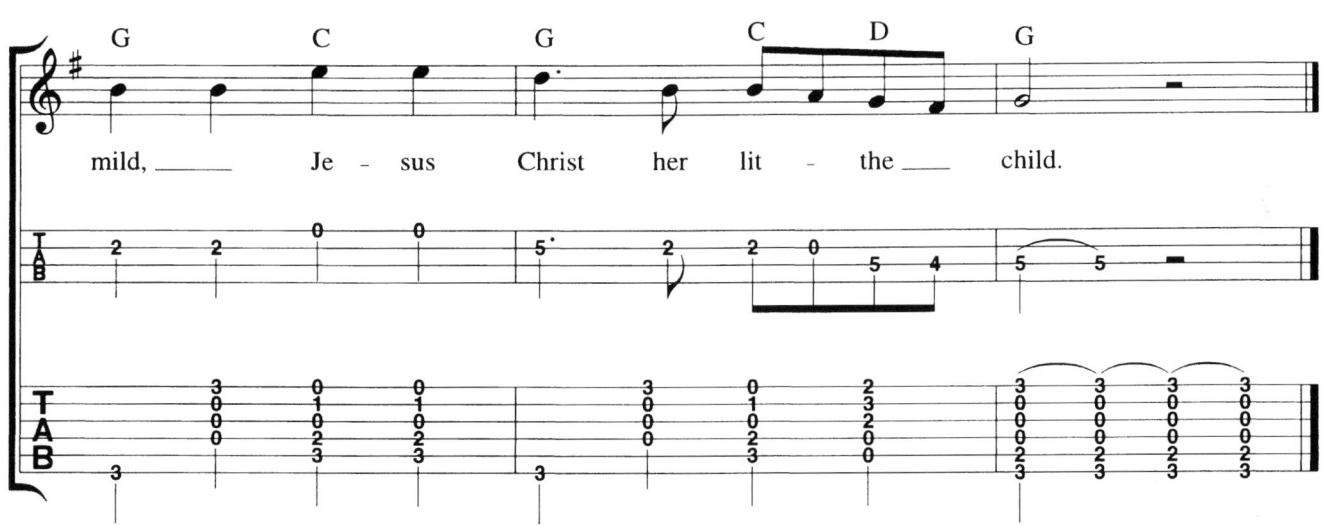

ONCE IN ROYAL DAVID'S CITY

Arr. by Steve Kaufman

1. Once in Royal David's city
   Stood a lowly cattle shed,
   Where a mother laid her baby
   In a manger for his bed:
   Mary was that mother mild,
   Jesus Christ her little child.

2. He came down to earth from heaven
   Who is God and Lord of all,
   And his shelter was a stable,
   And his cradle was a stall;
   With the poor and mean and lowly,
   Lived on earth our Savior holy.

3. And through all his wondrous childhood
   He would honor and obey,
   Love and watch the lowly maiden,
   In whose gentle arms he lay'
   Christian children all must be
   Mild obedient good as he.

4. For he is our childhood's pattern,
   Day by day like us he grew,
   He was little, weak and helpless,
   Tears and smiles like us he knew;
   And he feeleth for our sadness,
   And he shareth in our gladness.

5. And our eyes at last shall see him,
   Through his own redeeming love,
   For that child so dear and gentle
   Is our Lord in heaven above;
   And he leads his children on
   To the place where he is gone.

6. Not in that poor lowly stable,
   With the oxen standing by,
   We shall see him; but in heaven,
   See at God's right hand on high;
   Where like stars his children crowned
   All in white shall wait around.

O LITTLE TOWN OF BETHLEHEM

Phillips Brooks, 1868

Arr. by Steve Kaufman
L.H. Redner, 1868

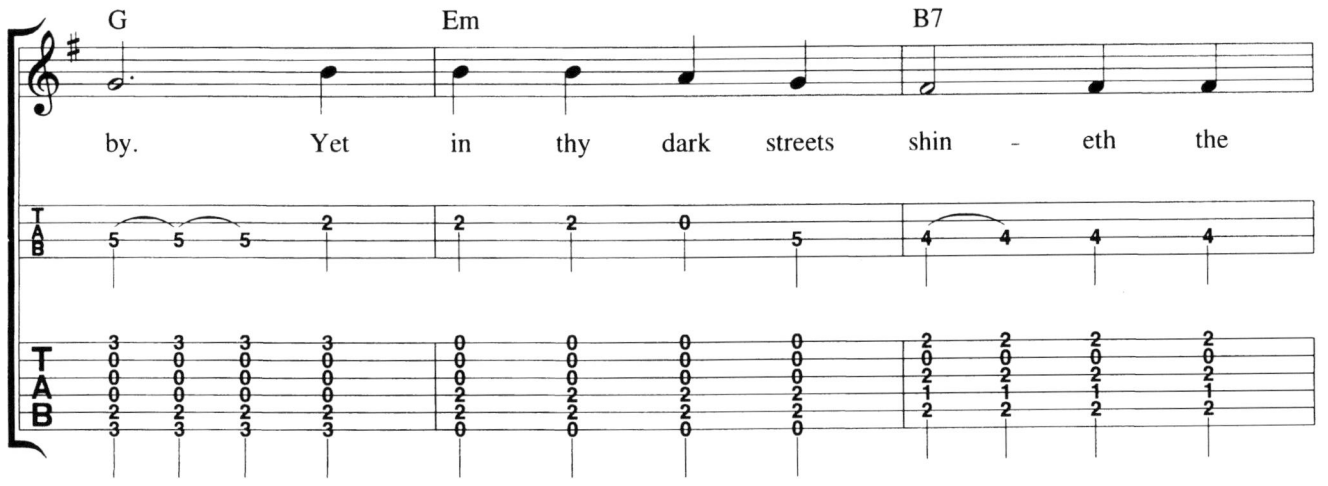
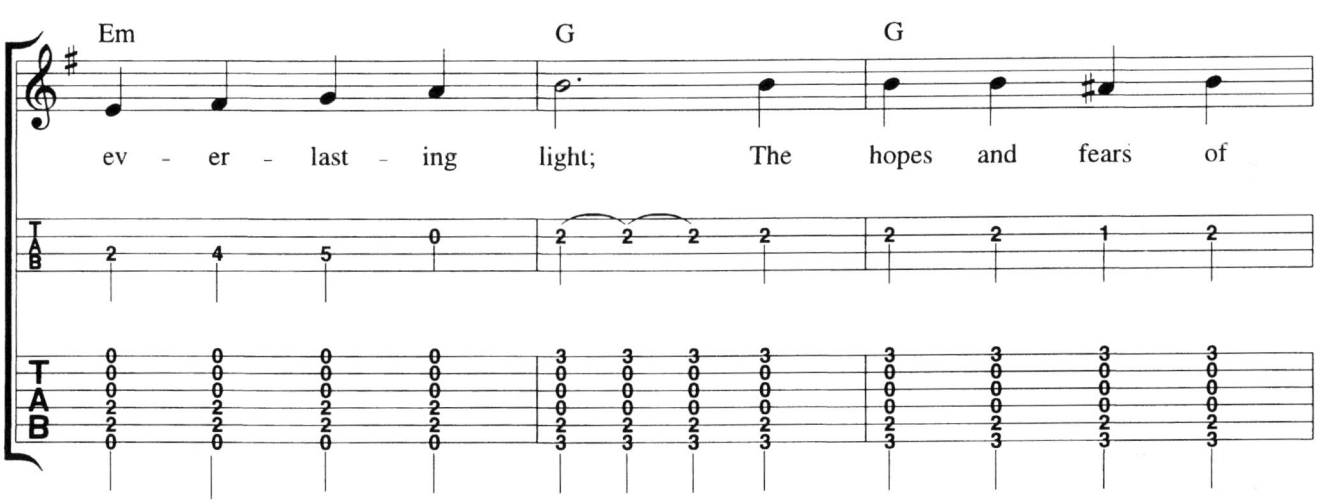
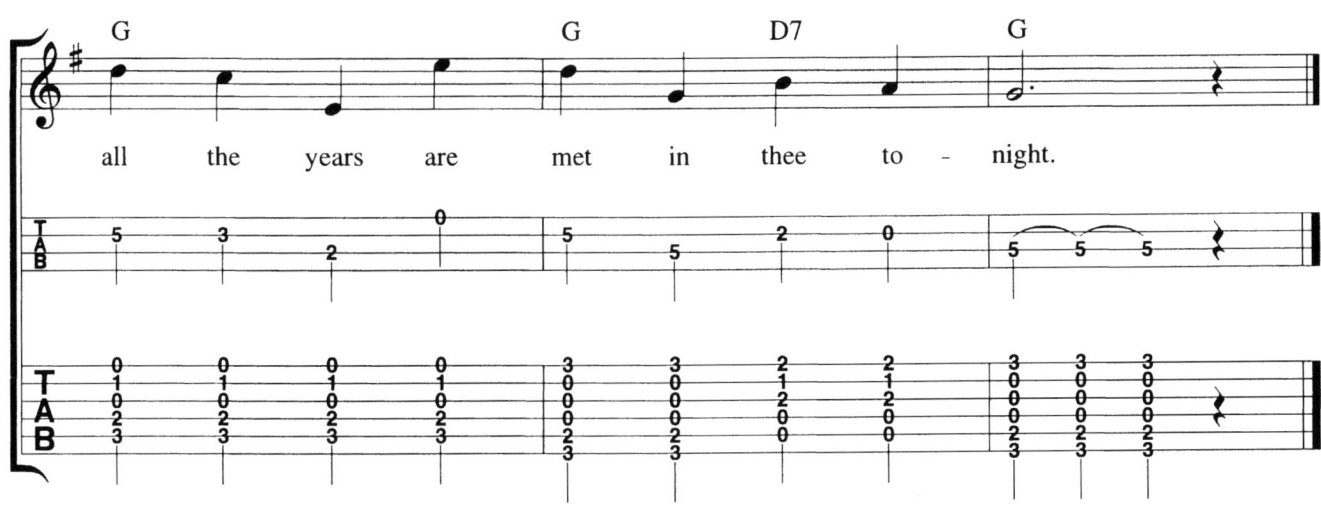

O LITTLE TOWN OF BETHLEHEM

3rd Solo

Arr. by Steve Kaufman

1. O little town of Bethlehem,
   How still we see thee lie!
   Above thy deep and dreamless sleep
   The silent stars go by;
   Yet in thy dark streets shineth
   The everlasting Light'
   The hopes and fears of all the years
   Are met in thee tonight.

2. For Christ is born of Mary,
   And, gathered all above.
   While mortals sleep, the angels keep
   Their watch of wondering love.
   O morning stars, together
   Proclaim the holy birth,
   And praises sing to God the King,
   And peace to men on Earth!

3. How silently, how silently
   The wondrous gift is given!
   So God imparts to human hearts
   The blessings of His heaven.
   No ear may hear his coming,
   But in this world of sin,
   Where meek souls will receive Him, still
   The dear Christ enters in.

4. O holy child of Bethlehem!
   Descend to us, we pray;
   Cast out our sin and enter in;
   Be born in us today.
   We hear the Christmas angels
   The great glad tidings tell;
   O come to us, abide with us,
   Our Lord Immanuel!

JOY TO THE WORLD

Isaac Watts

Arr. by Steve Kaufman
George F. Handel

82

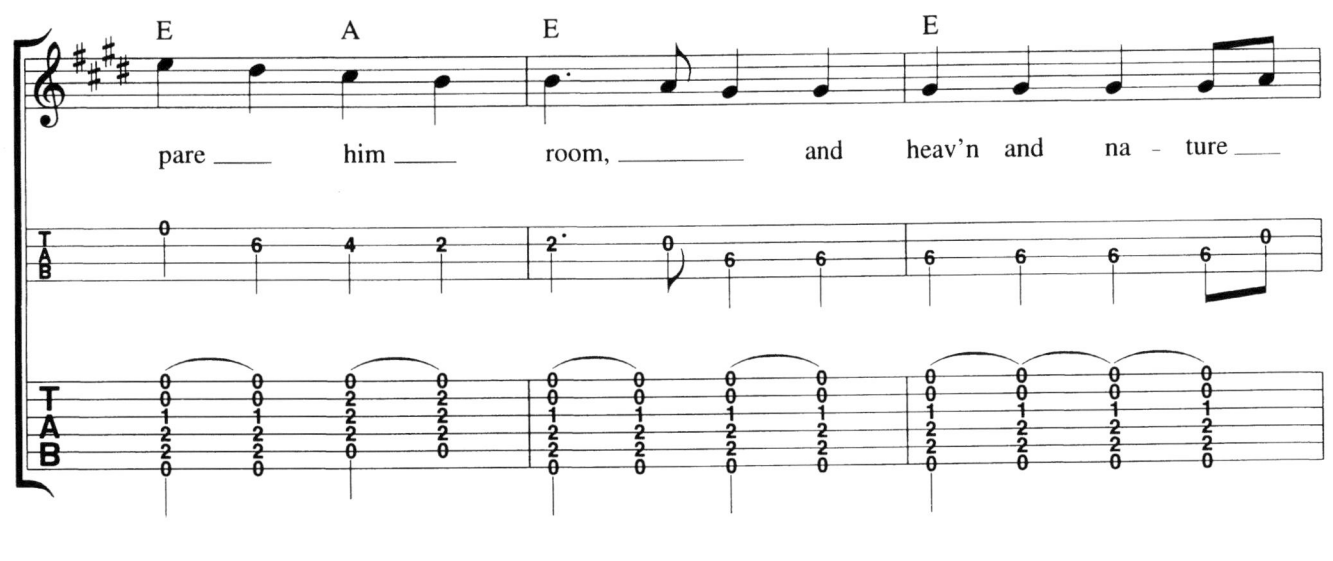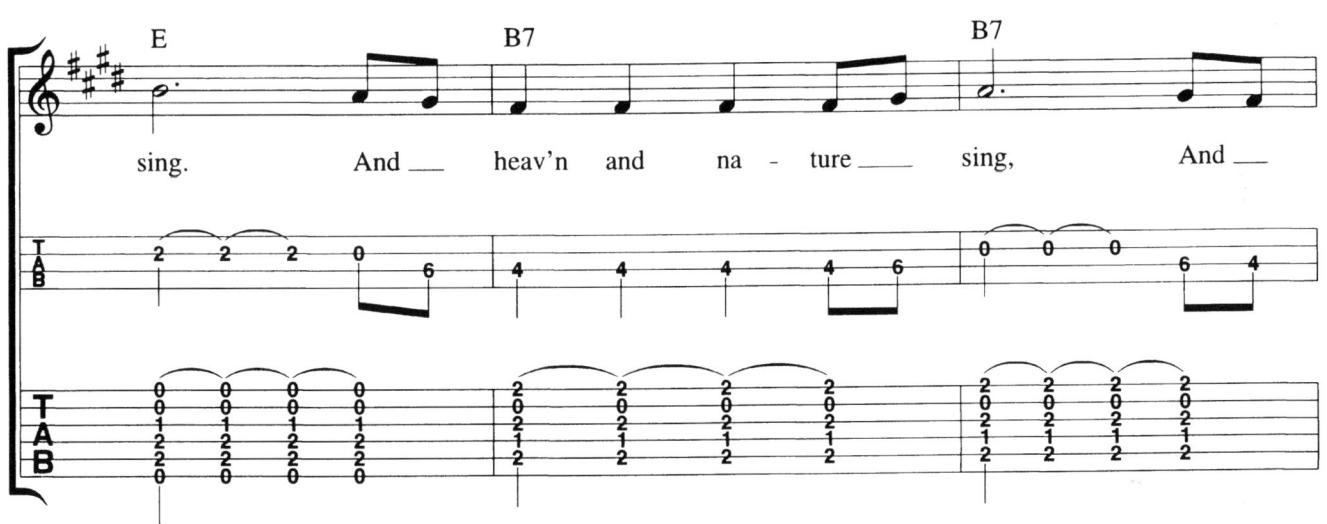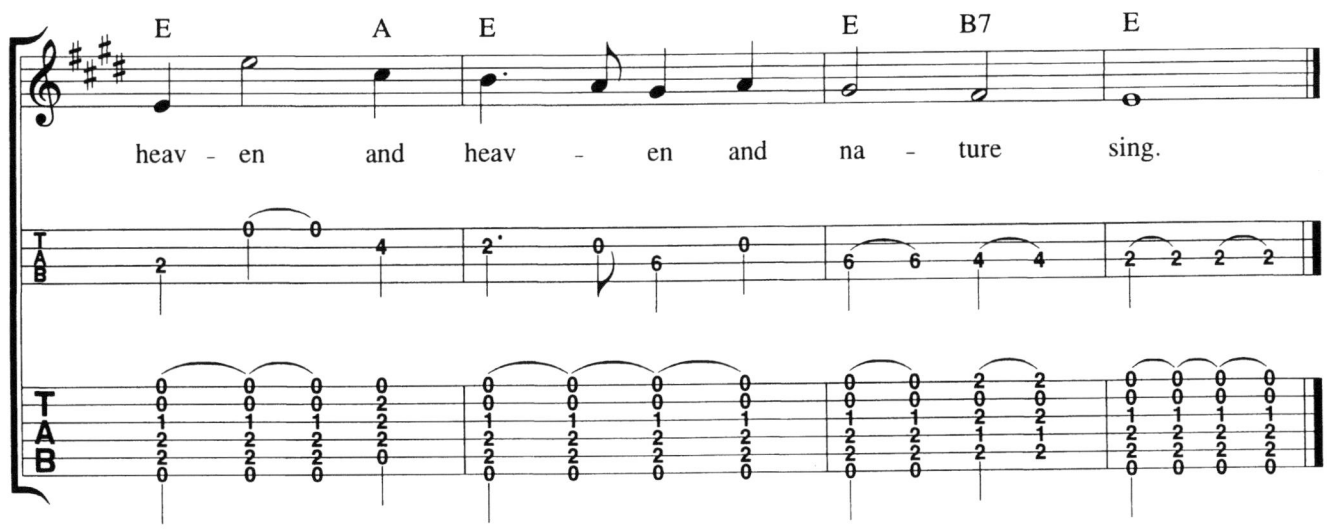

JOY TO THE WORLD

Arr. by Steve Kaufman

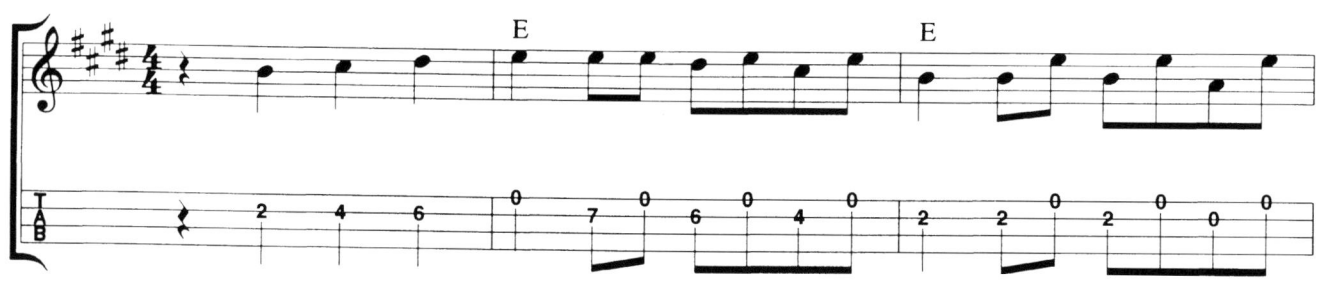

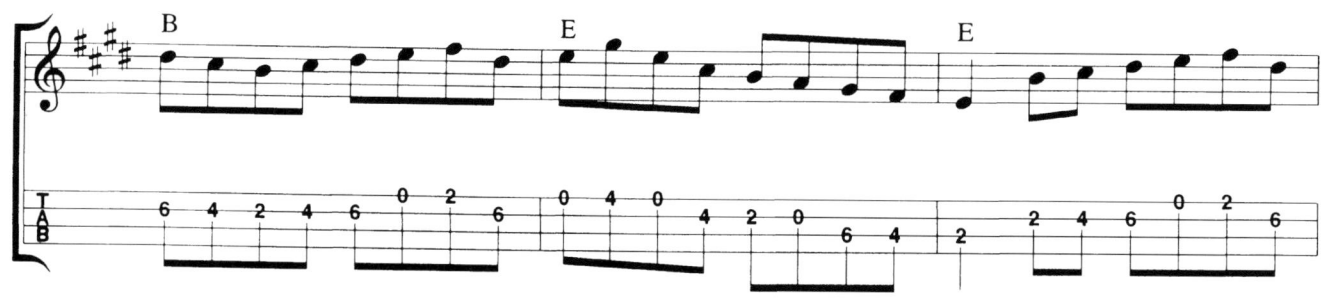
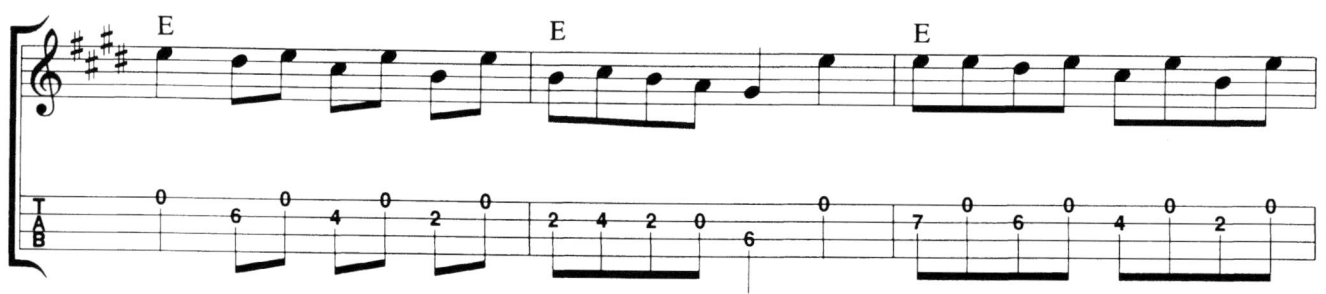

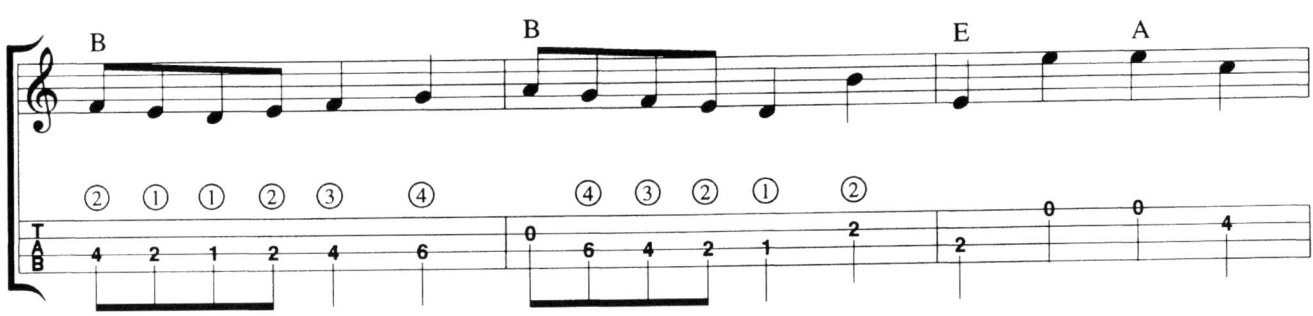

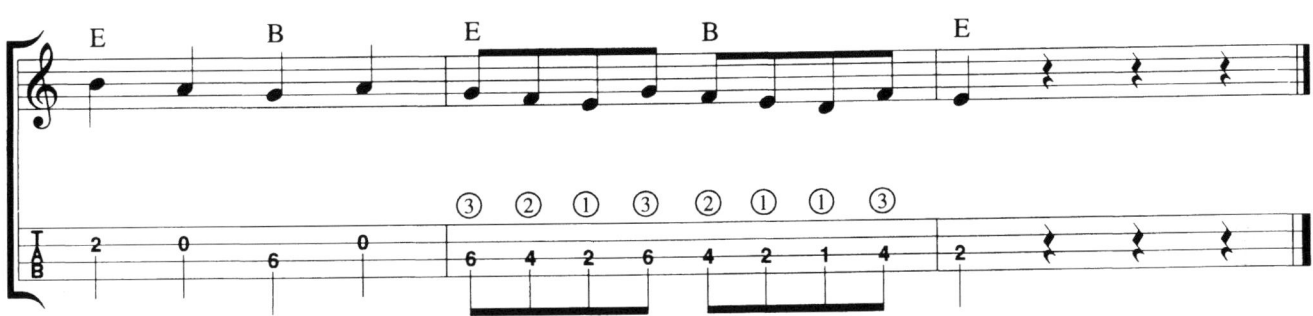

1. Joy to the world! The Lord has come!
   Let Earth receive her King;
   Let every heart prepare Him room,
   And heav'n and nature sing,
   And heav'n and nature sing,
   And heav'n, and heav'n and nature
     sing.

2. Joy to the world! The Savior reigns;
   Let men their songs employ;
   While fields and floods, rocks, hills
     and plains
   Repeat the sounding joy,
   Repeat the sounding joy,
   Repeat, repeat the sounding joy.

3. He rules the world with truth and grace,
   And makes the nations prove;
   The glories of His righteousness
   And wonders of His love,
   And wonders of His love,
   And wonders, and wonders of His love.

AULD LANG SYNE

Arr. by Steve Kaufman

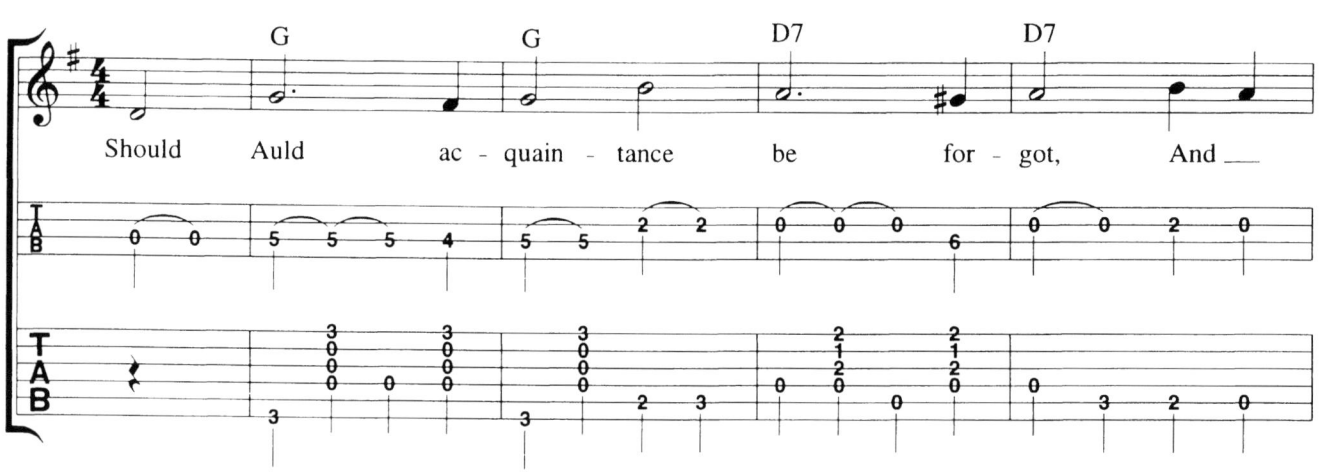
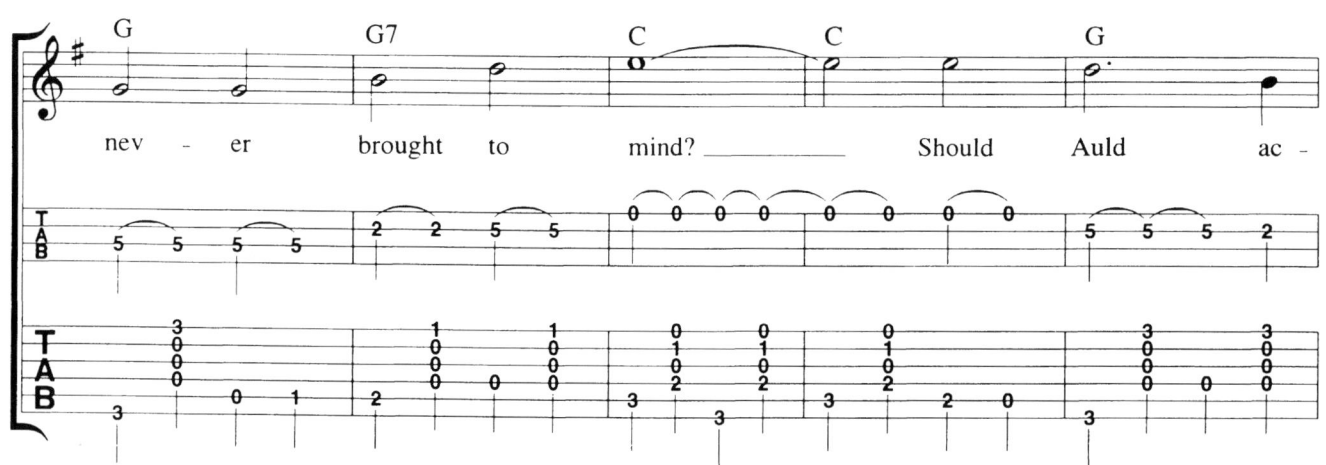
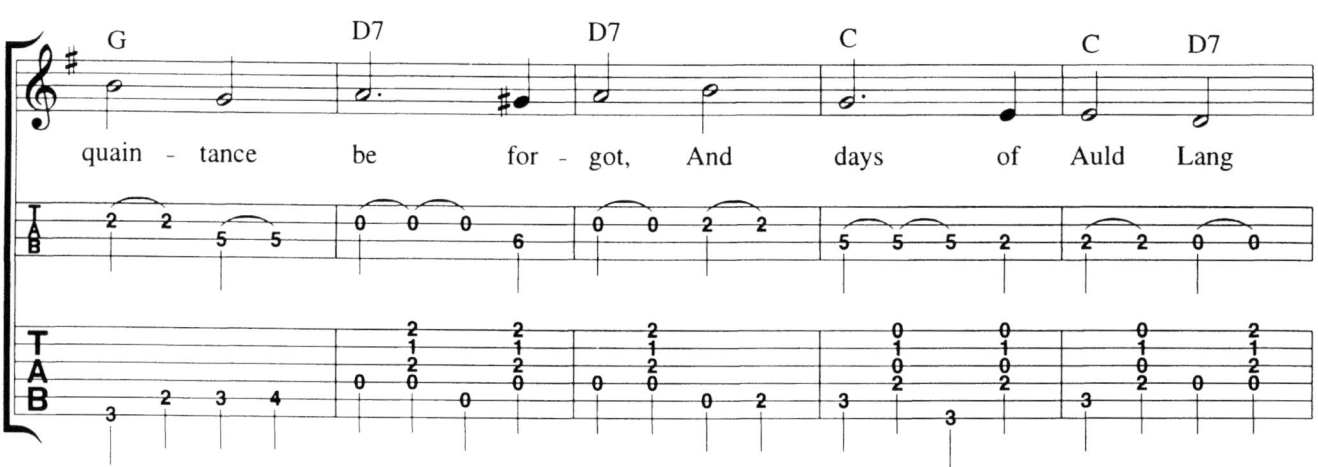

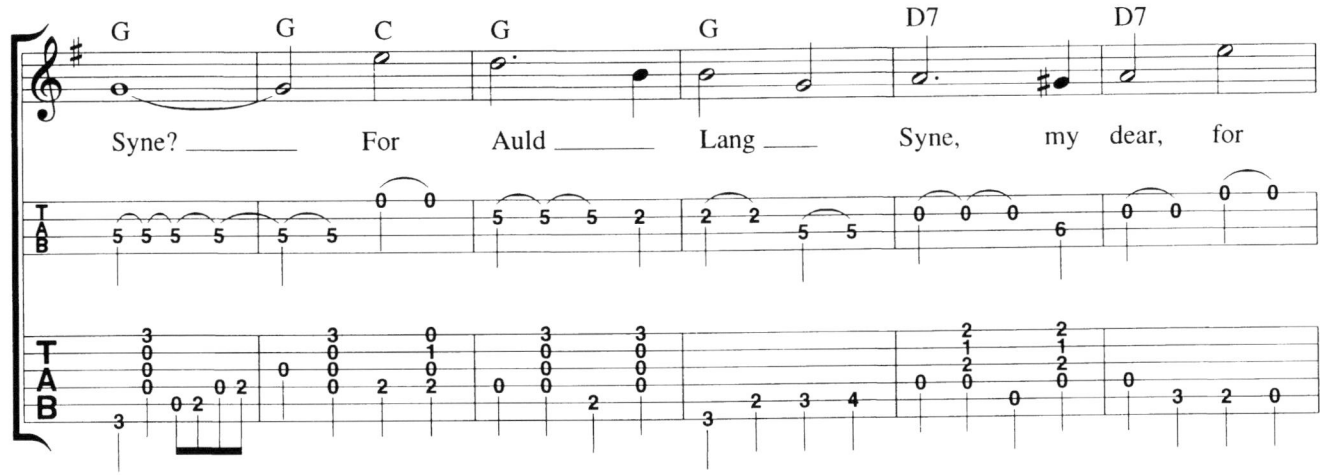
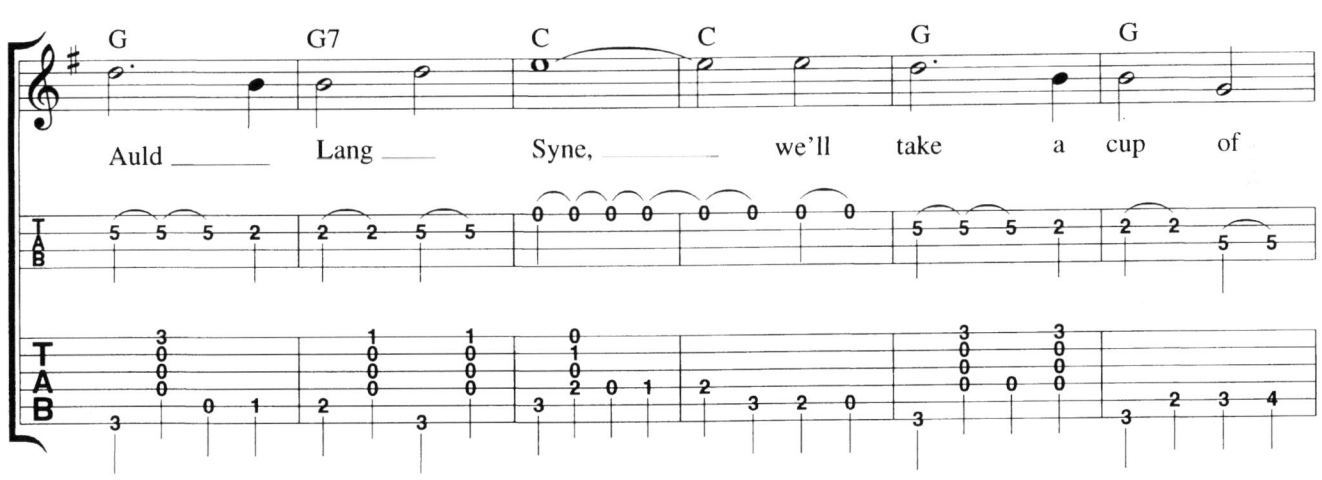
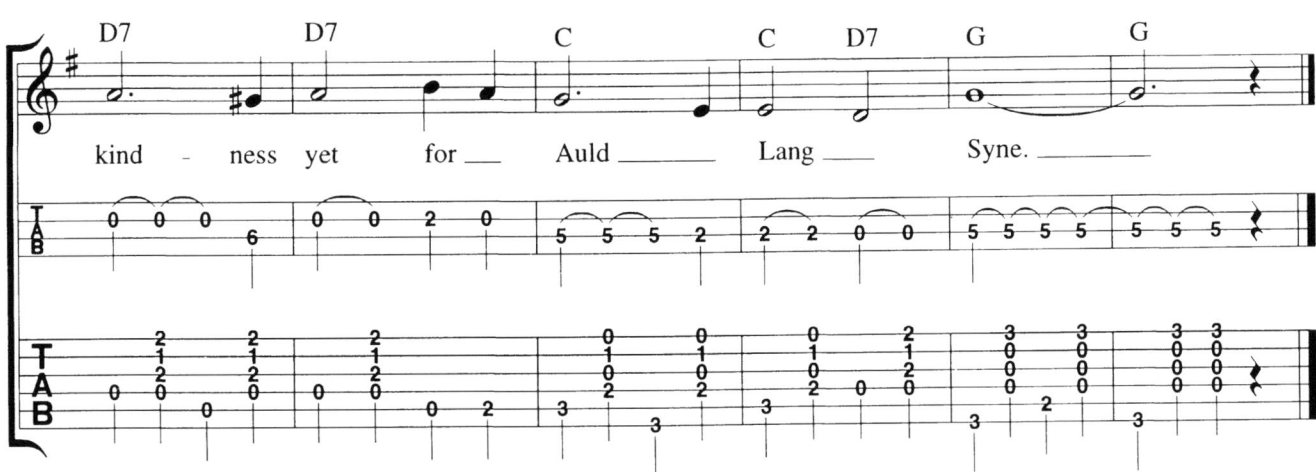

AULD LANG SYNE

Arr. by Steve Kaufman

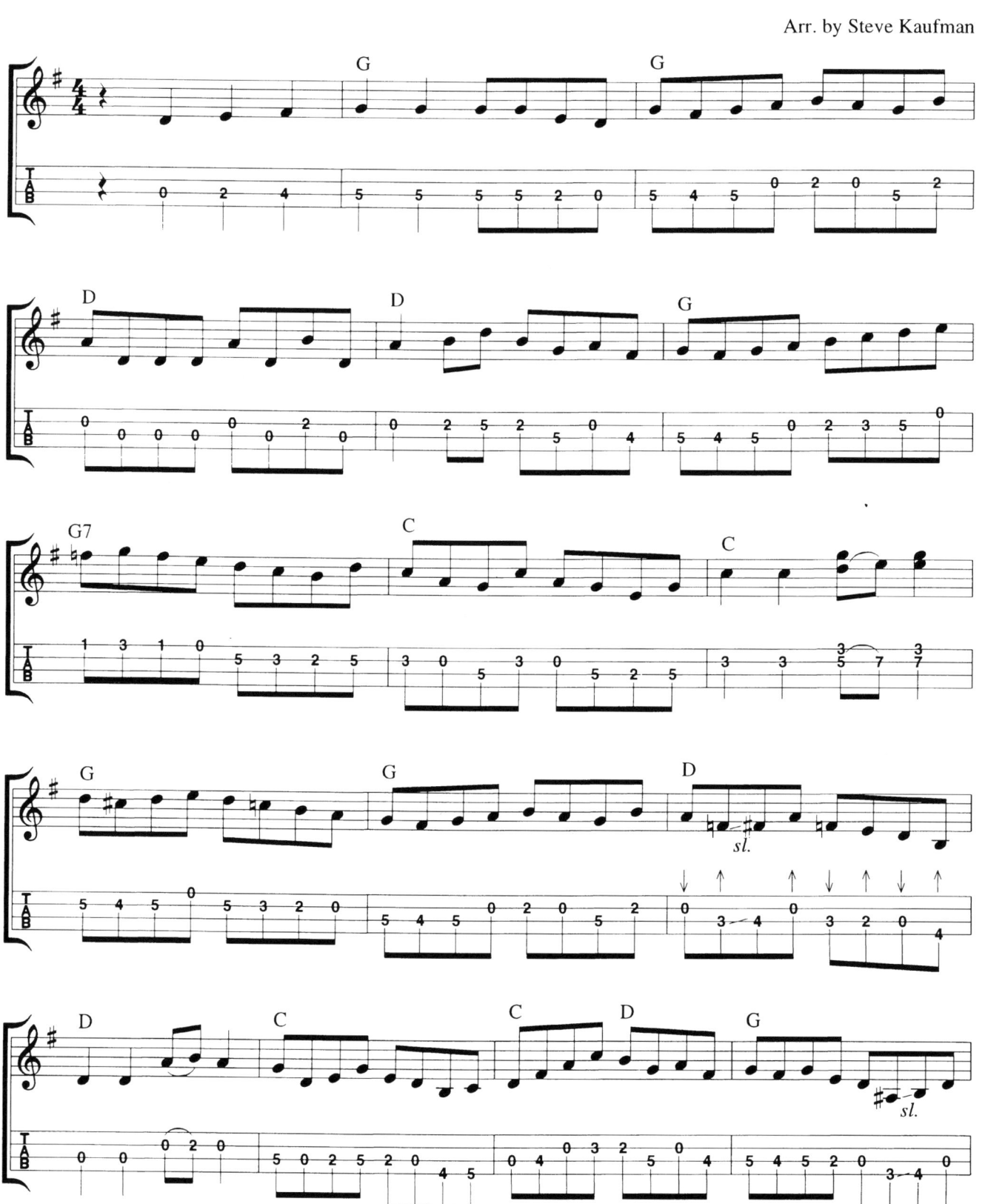

1. Should Auld acquaintance be forgot,
And never brought to mind?
Should Auld acquaintance be forgot,
And days of Auld Lang Syne?

Chorus
For Auld Lang Syne, my dear,
For Auld Lang Syne;
We'll take a cup o' kindness yet
For Auld Lang Syne.

2. And here's a hand, my trusty friend,
And give's a hand o' thine;
We'll take a cup o' kindness yet
For Auld Lang Syne.

THE GOLDEN CAROL
of Melchior, Casper and Balthazar

Arr. by Steve Kaufman

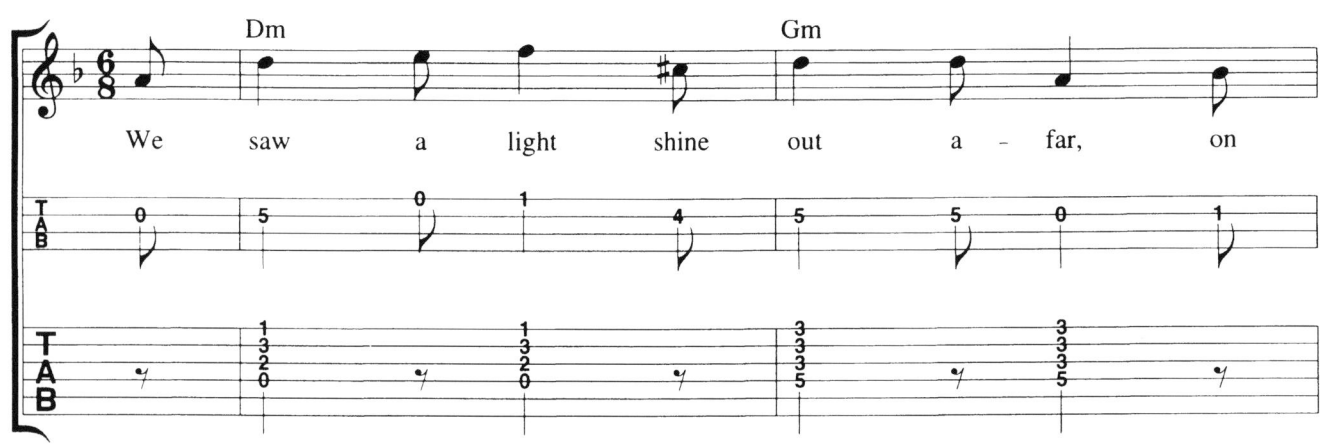

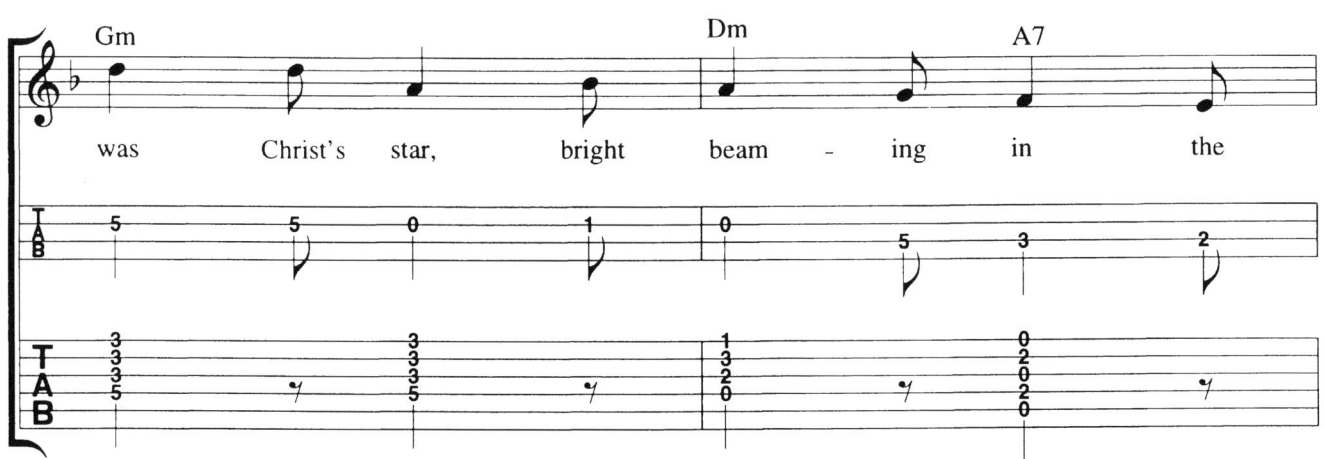

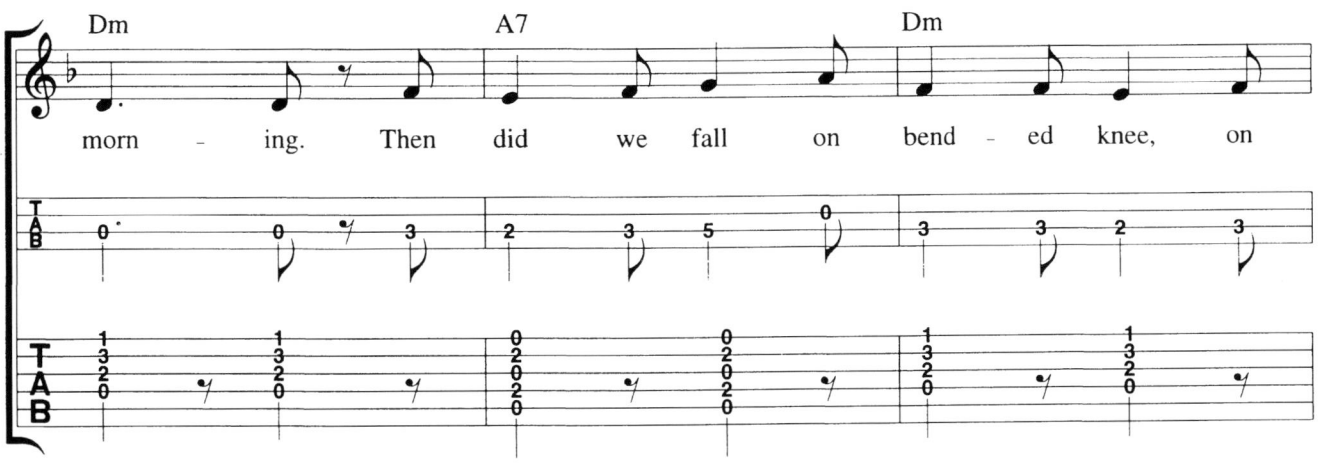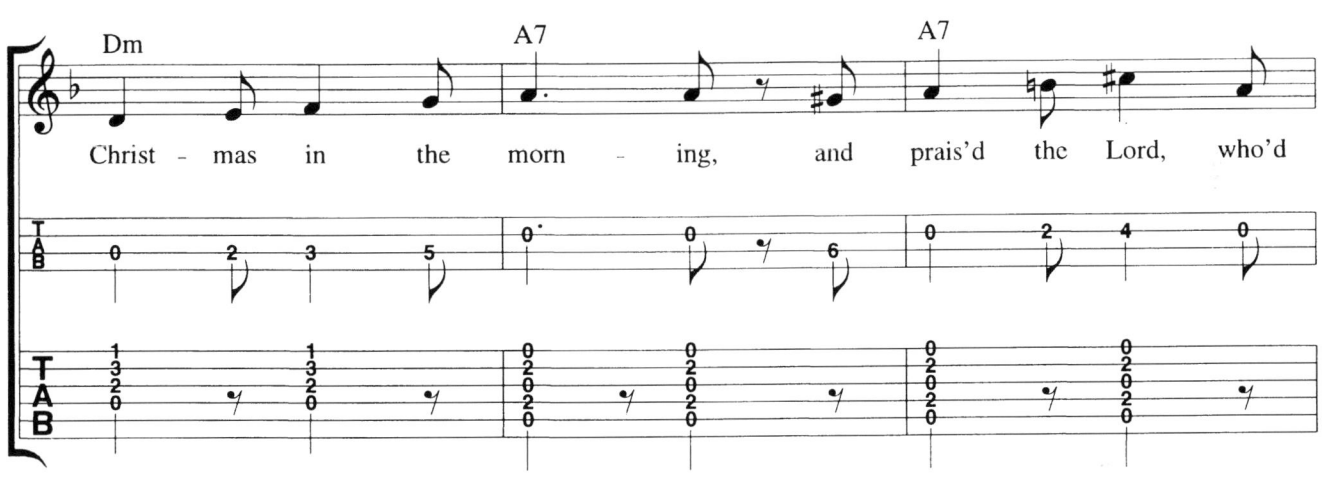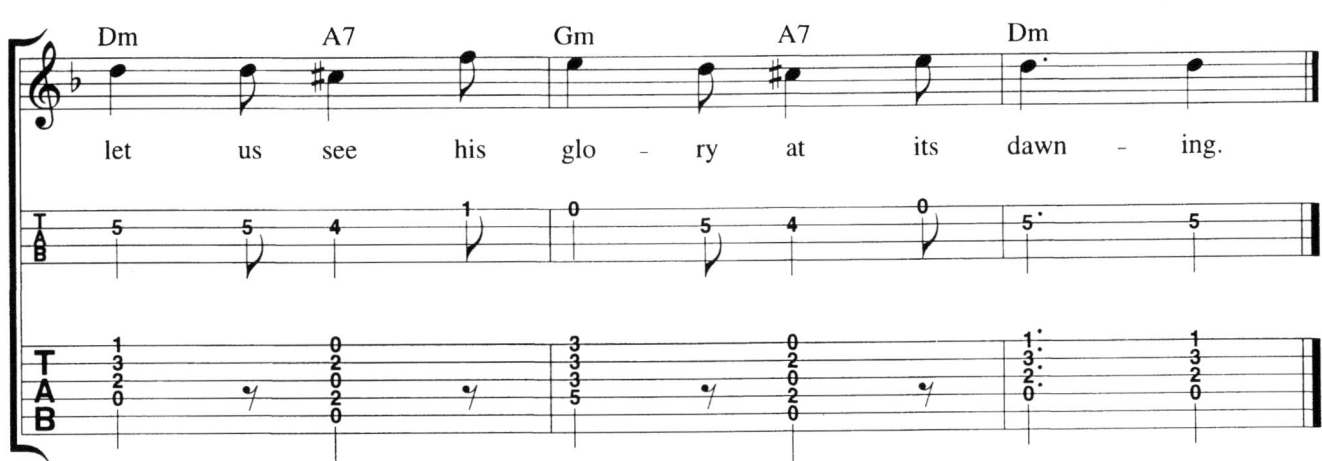

THE GOLDEN CAROL

Arr. by Steve Kaufman

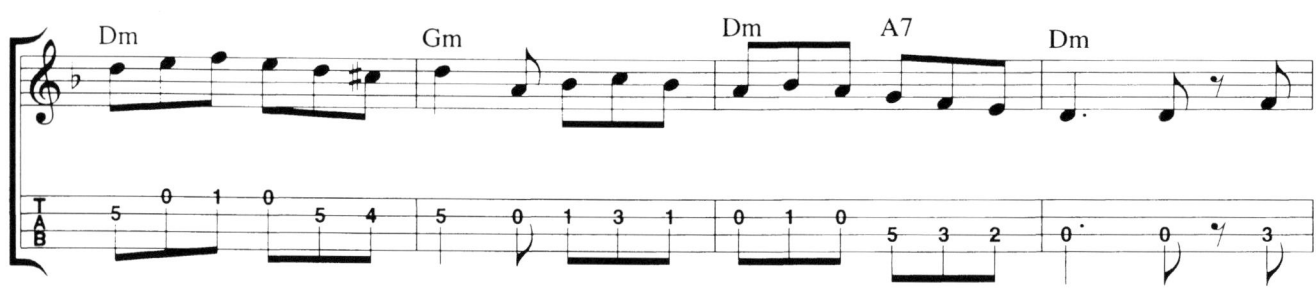
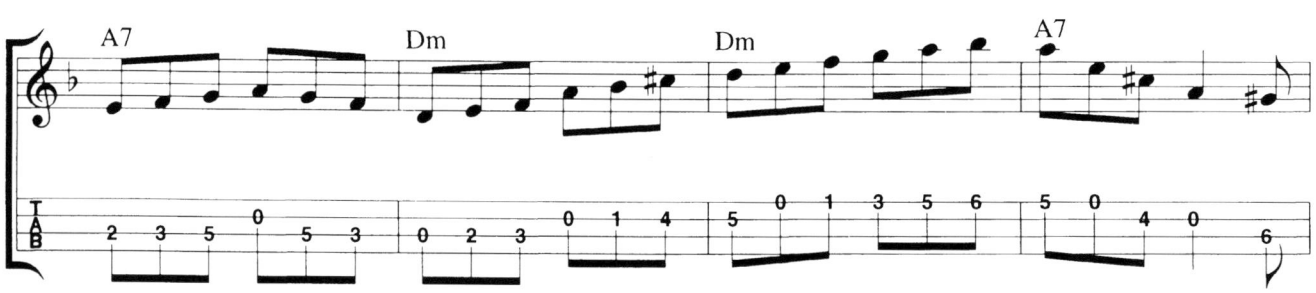
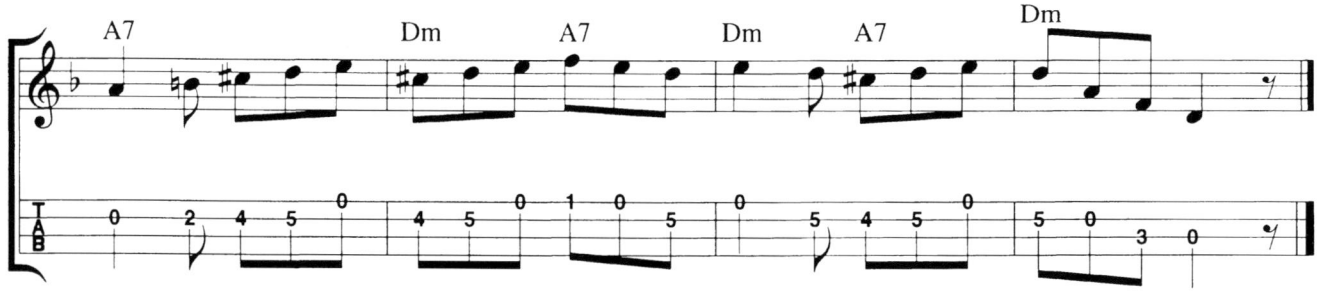

1. We saw a light shine out afar,
   On Christmas in the morning,
   And straight we knew it was Christ's star,
   Bright beaming morning.
   Then did we fall on bended knee,
   On Christmas in the morning,
   And prais'd the Lord, who'd let us see
   His glory at its dawning.

2. Oh! ever thought be His name,
   On Christmas in the morning,
   Who bore for us both grief and shame,
   Afflictions sharpest scorning.
   And may we die, when death shall come,
   On Christmas in the morning,
   And see in heav'n, our glorious home,
   That Star of Christmas morning.

STAR IN THE EAST

Arr. by Steve Kaufman

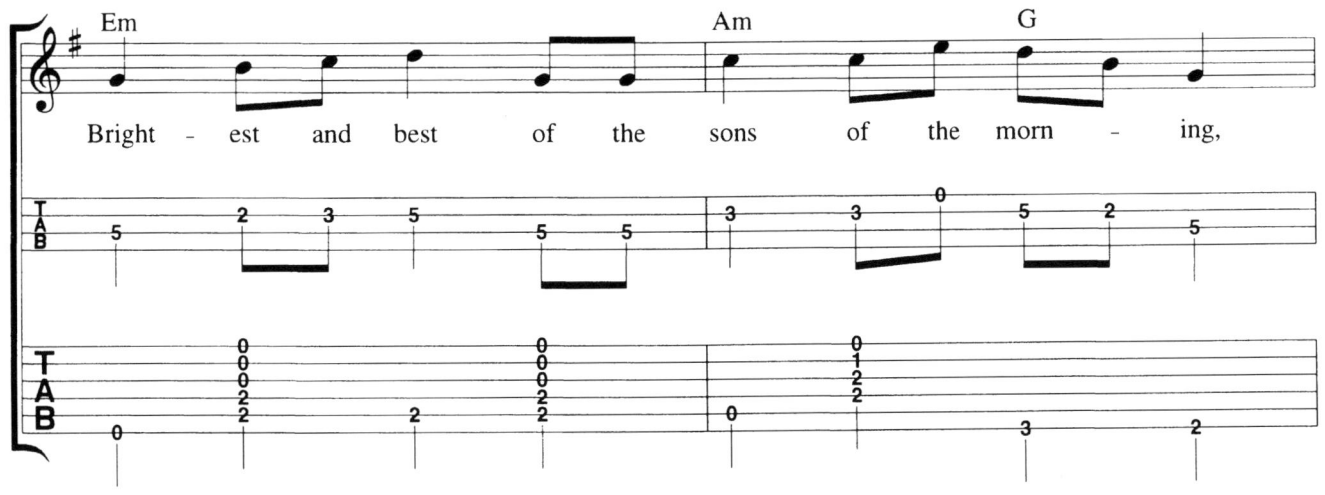
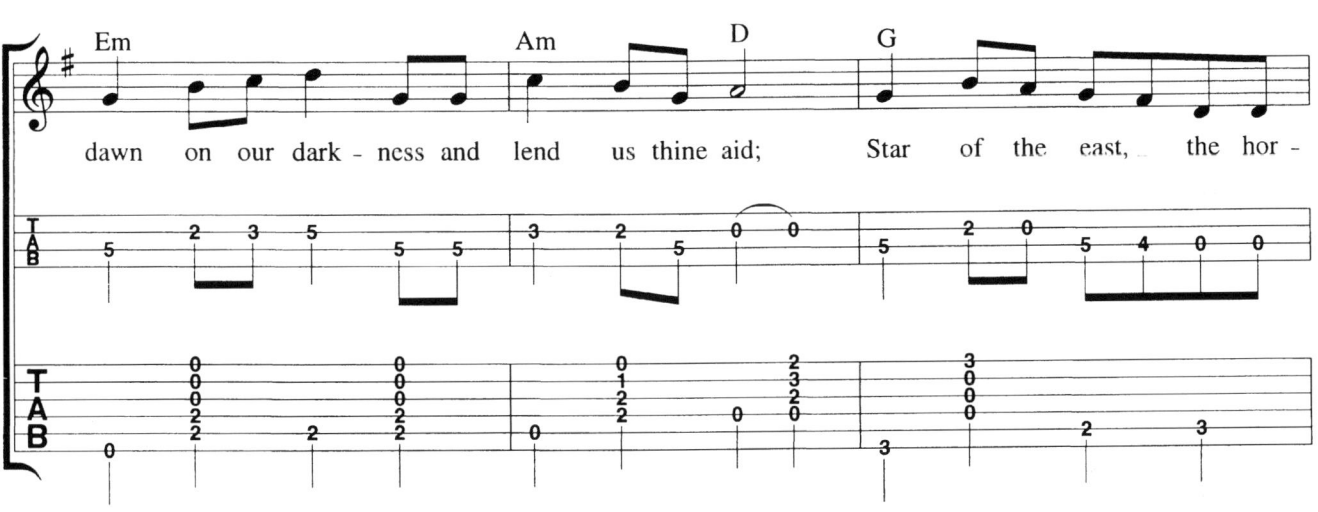

STAR IN THE EAST

Arr. by Steve Kaufman

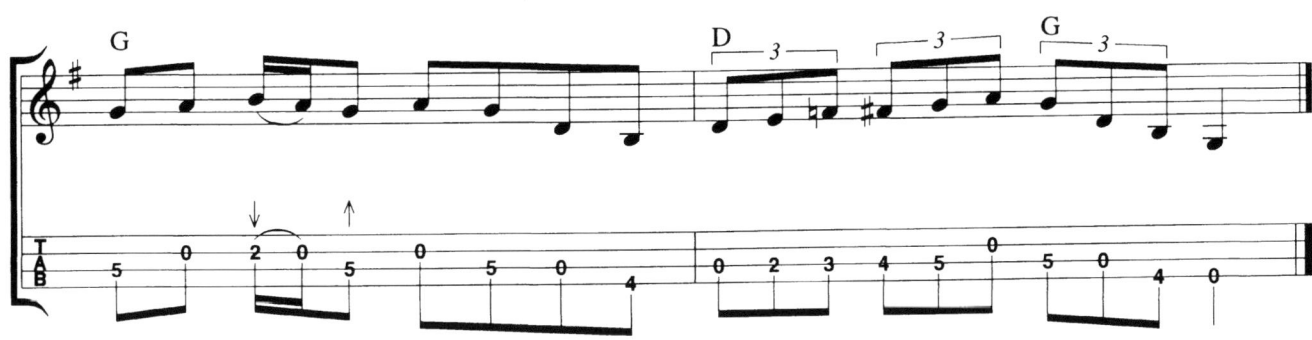

1. Hail, blessed morn! See the great mediator
   Down from the regions of glory descend!
   Shepherds, go worship the Babe in the manger,
   Lo, for a guard the bright angels attend.

   Chorus
   Brightest and the best of the sons of the morning,
   Dawn on our darkness and lend us Thine aid;
   Star of the East, the horizon adorning,
   Guide where our infant Redeemer is laid.

2. Cold on his cradle the dew-drops are shining,
   Low lies his head with the beasts of the stall;
   Angels adore him in slumber reclining,
   Maker and monarch and Saviour of all.
   Chorus

3. Say, shall we not yield him in costly devotion,
   Odors of Edom, and off'rings divine,
   Gems of the mountain and pearls of the ocean,
   Myrrh from the forest, and gold from the mine?
   Chorus

4. Vainly we offer each ample oblation,
   Vainly with gifts would his favor secure;
   Richer by far is the heart's adoration,
   Dearer to God are the prayers of the poor.
   Chorus

5. Low at his feet we in humble prostration,
   Lose all our sorrow and trouble and strife;
   There we receive his divine consolation,
   Flowing afresh from the fountain of life.
   Chorus

6. He is our friend in the midst of temptation,
   Faithful supporter, whose love cannot fail;
   Rock of our refuge, and hope of salvation,
   Light to direct us through death's gloomy vale.
   Chorus

7. Star of the morning, thy brightness, declining,
   Shortly must fade when the sun doth arise;
   Beaming refulgent, his glory eternal,
   Shines on the children of love in the skies.
   Chorus

DOWN IN YON FOREST

Arr. by Steve Kaufman

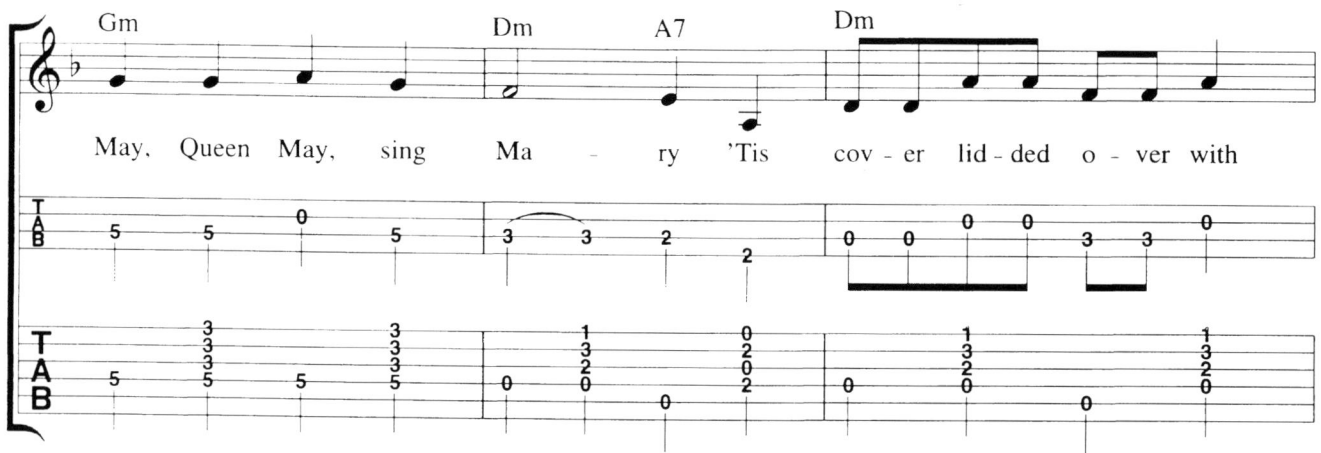
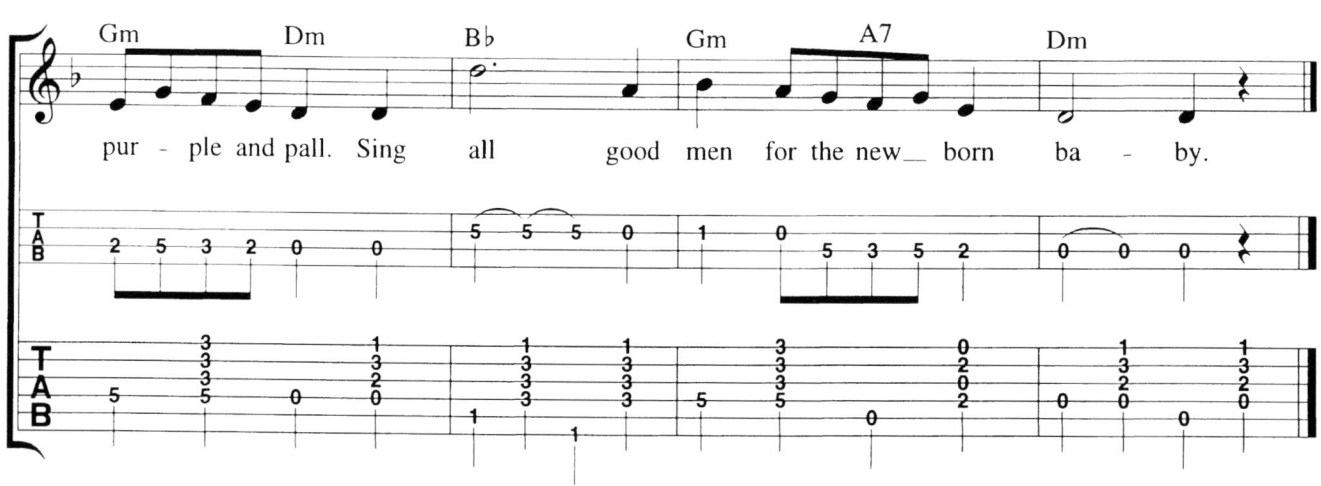

DOWN IN YON FOREST

Arr. by Steve Kaufman

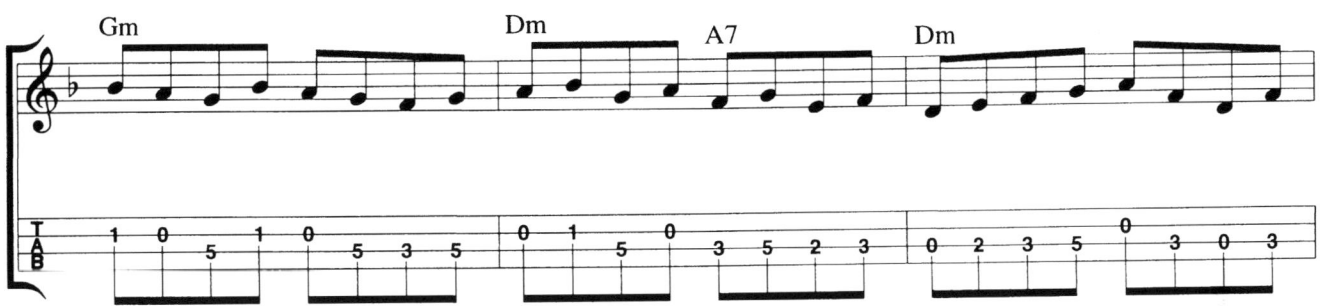

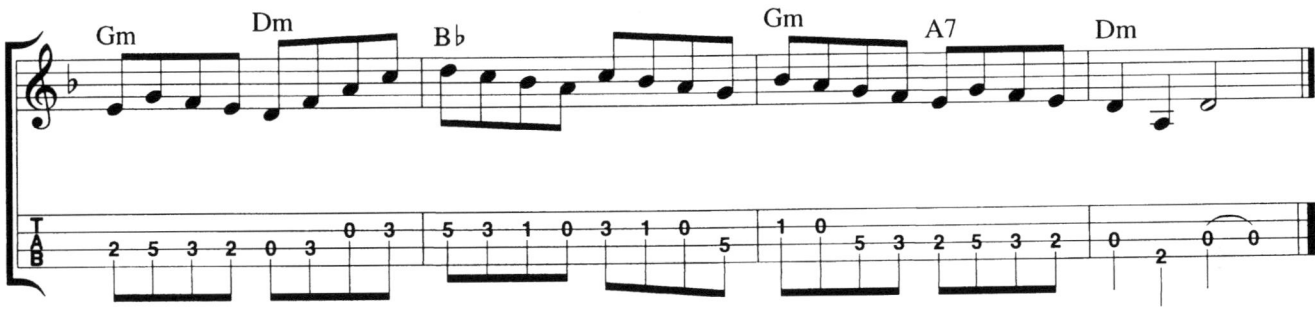

1. Down in yon forest be a hall,
   Sing May, Queen May, Sing Mary!
   'Tis cover lidded over with purple and pall.
   Sing all good men for the new-born baby!

2. Oh in that hall is a pallet bed,
   Sing May, Queen May, sing Mary!
   On which the virgin did atone
   Sing all good men for the new-born baby!

3. And at that pallet is a stone,
   Sing May, Queen May, sing Mary!
   On which the virgin did atone
   Sing all good men for the new-born baby!

4. Under that hall is a gushing flood;
   Sing May, Queen May, sing Mary!
   From Christ's own side, 'tis water and blood.
   Sing all good men for the new-born baby!

5. Beside that bed a shrub tree grows,
   Sing May, Queen May, sing Mary!
   Since he was born hit blooms and blows.
   Sing all good men for the new-born baby!

6. Oh, on that bed a young squire sleeps,
   Sing May, Queen May, sing Mary!
   His wounds are sick, and see, he weeps.
   Sing all good men for the new-born baby!

7. Oh hail yon hall where none can sin,
   Sing May, Queen May, sing Mary!
   Cause hit's gold outside and silver within,
   Sing all good men for the new-born baby!

AND THE TREES DO MOAN

Arr. by Steve Kaufman

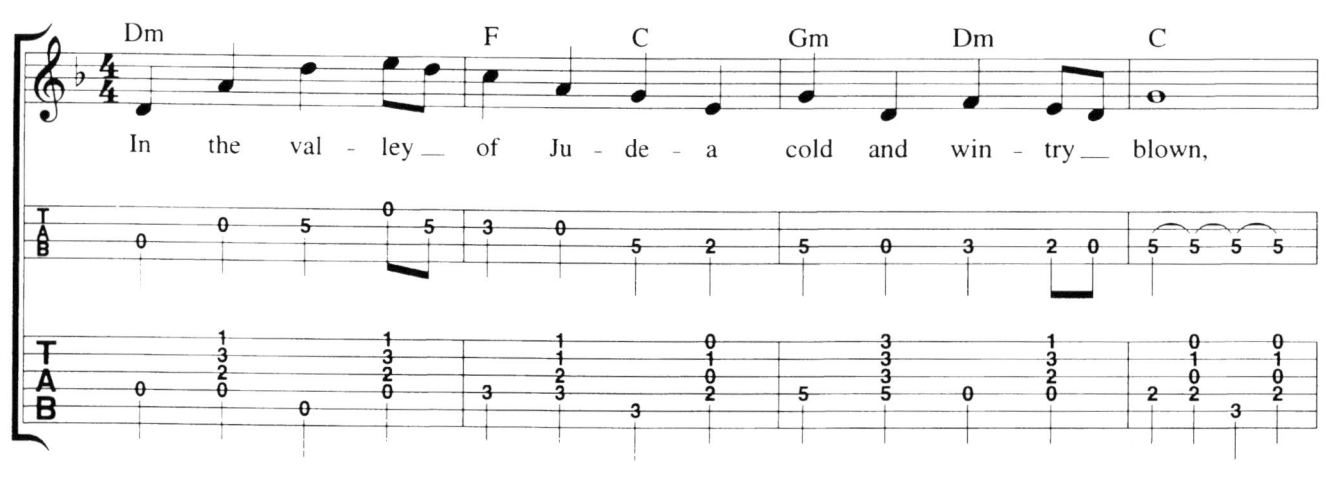

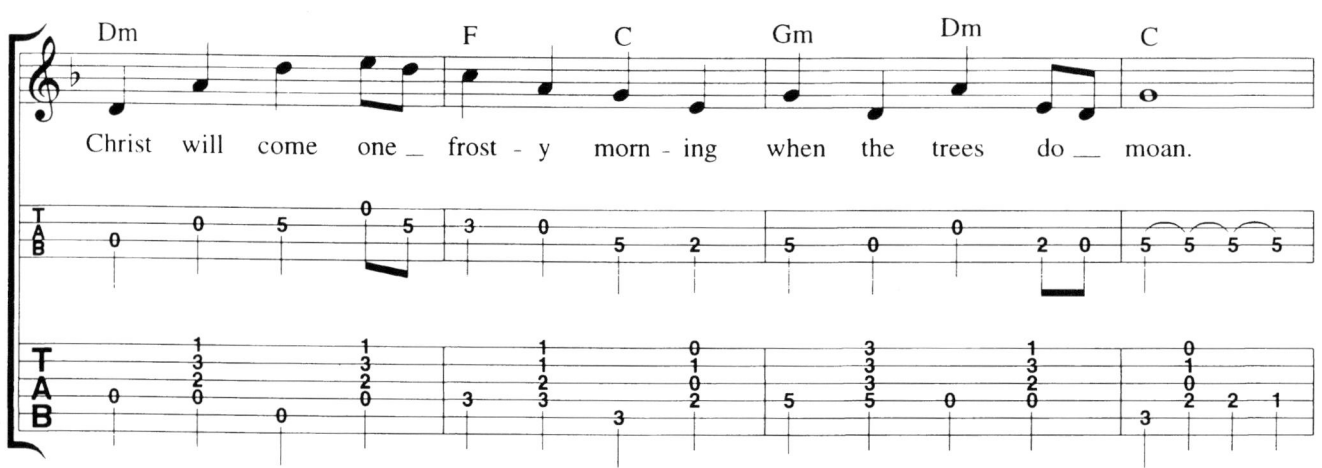

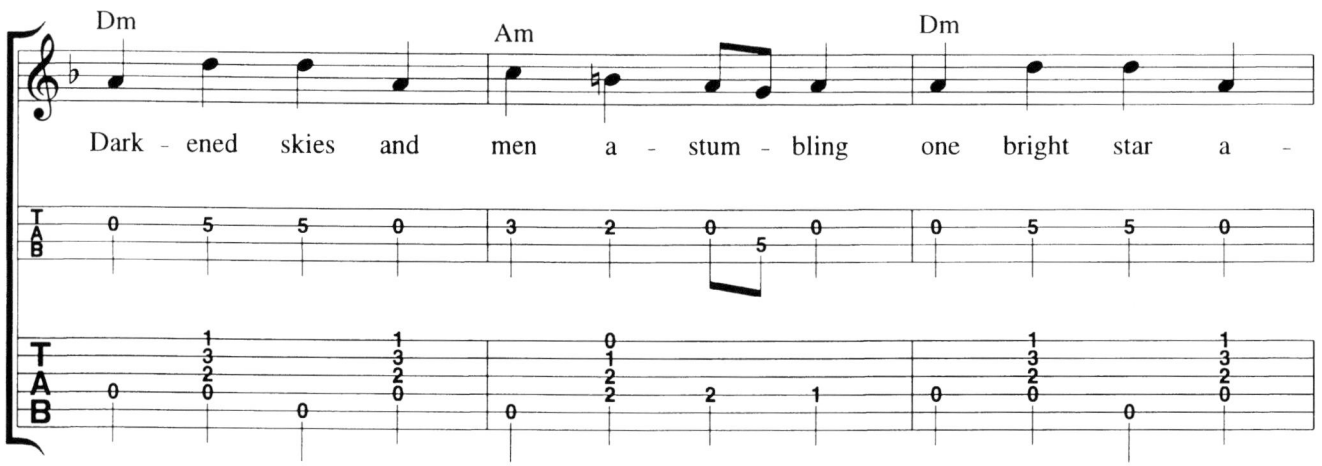

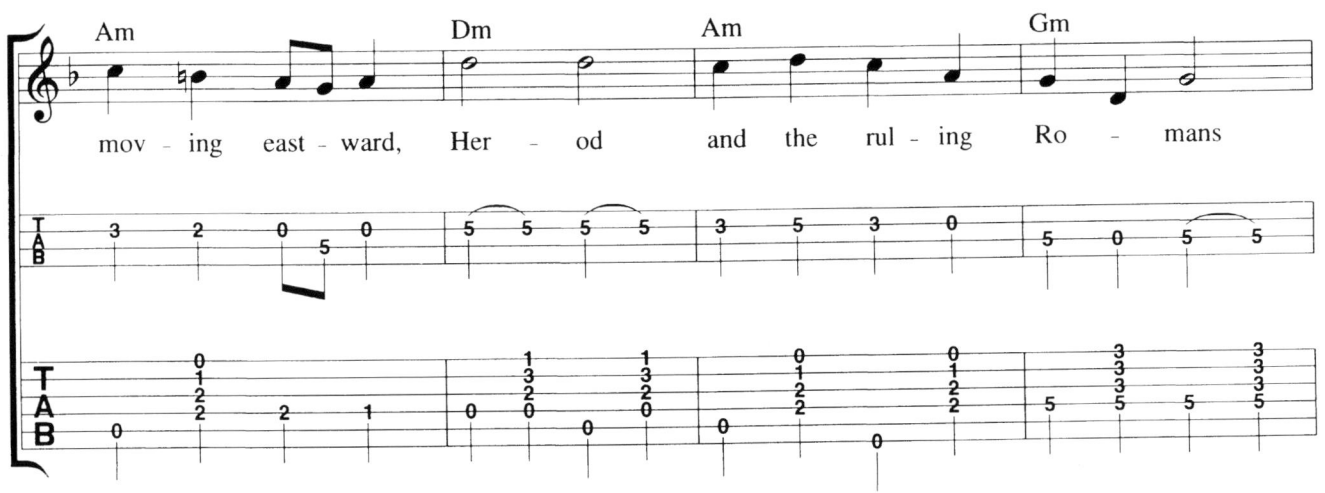
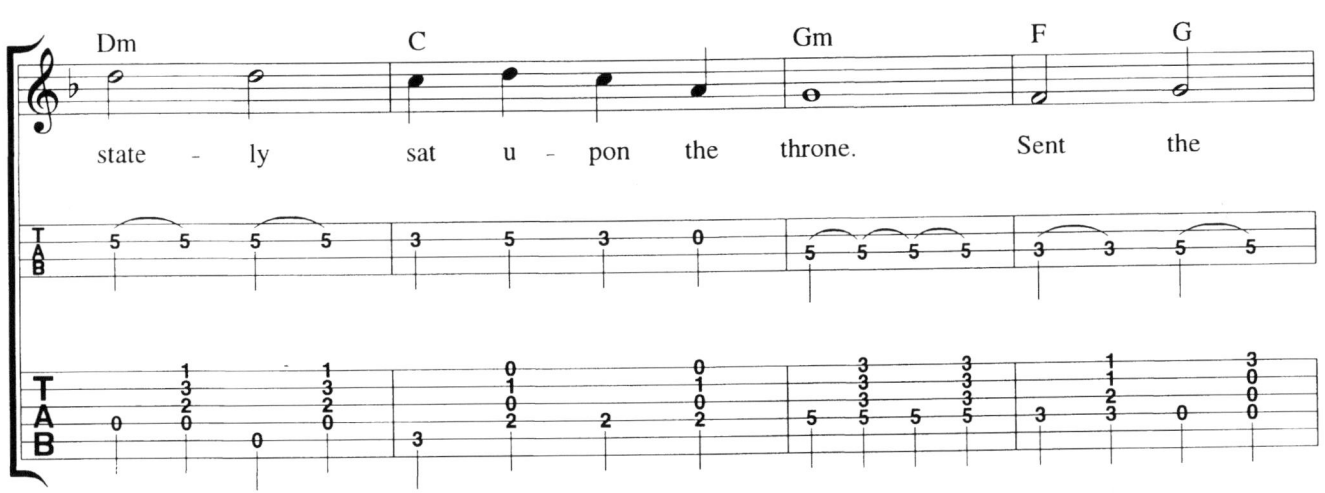
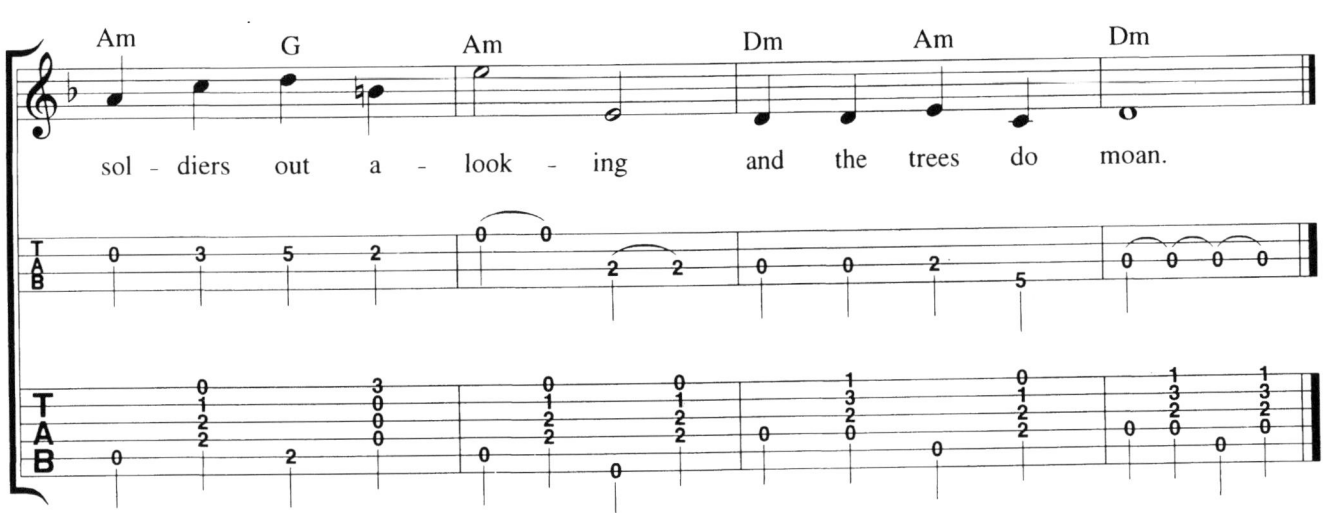

AND THE TREES DO MOAN

Arr. by Steve Kaufman

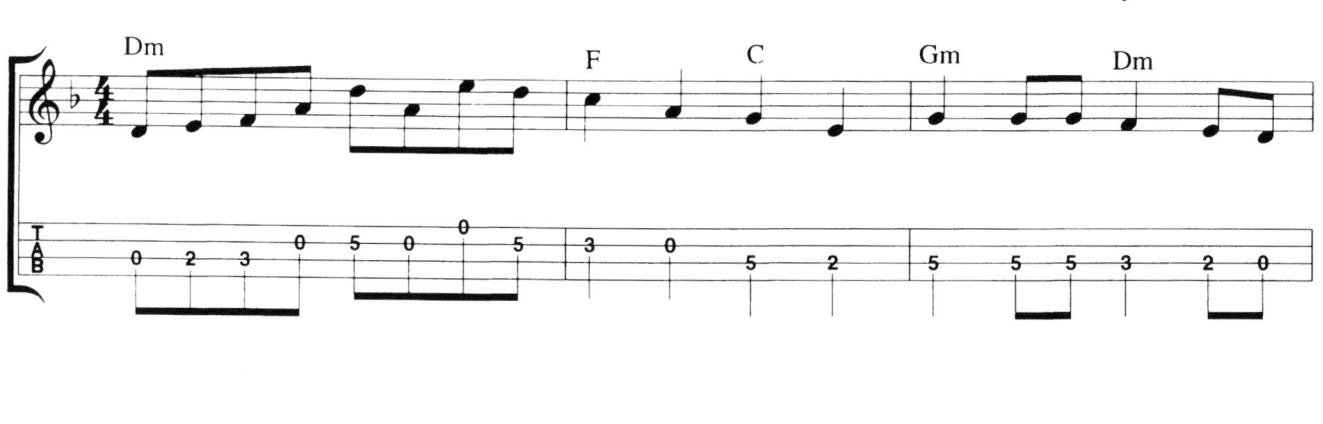
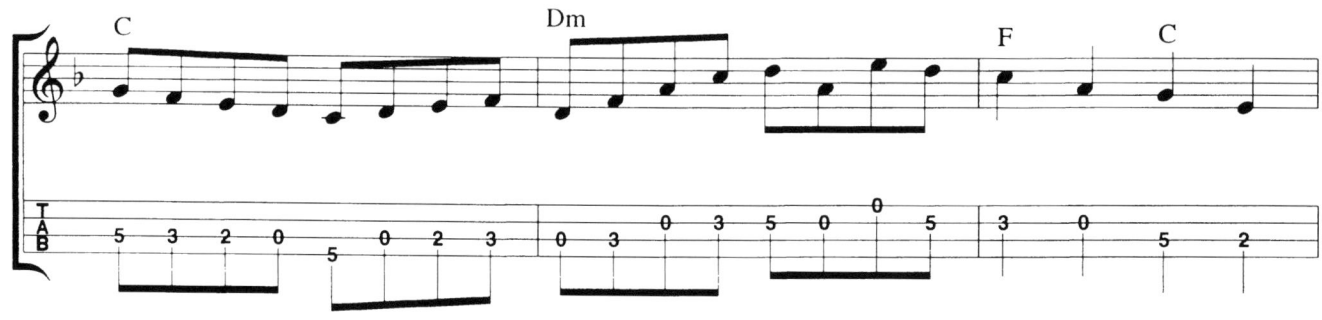
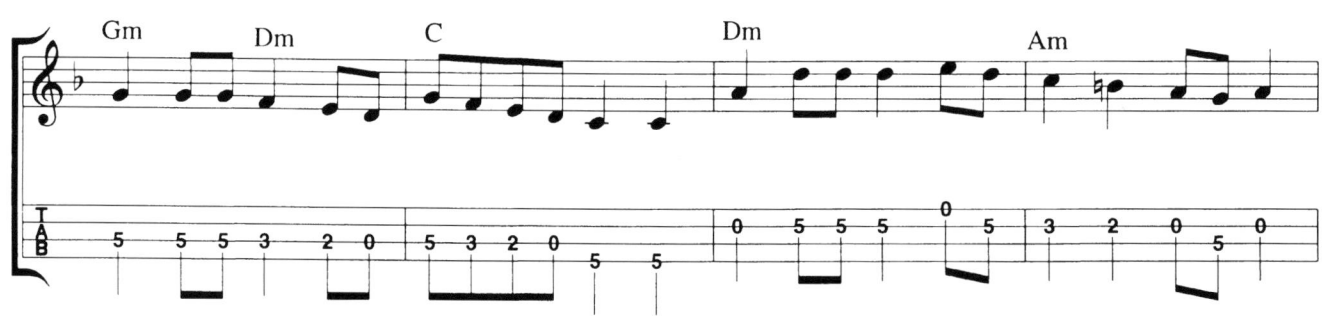
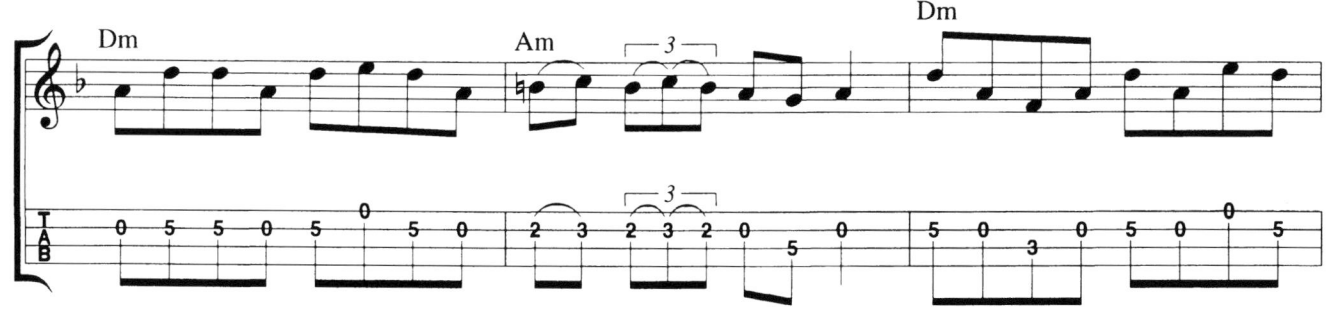

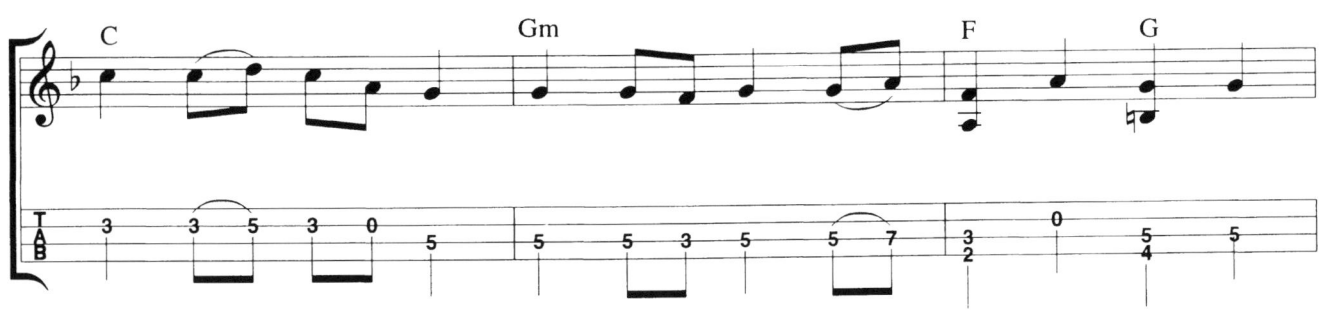

In the valley of Judea
cold and wintry blown,
Christ will come one frosty morning
when the trees do moan.

Darkened skies and men a-stumbling
one bright star a-moving eastward,
Herod and the ruling Romans
stately sat upon the throne.
Sent the solders out a-looking
and the trees do moan.

WHILE SHEPHERDS WATCHED THEIR FLOCKS

Arr. by Steve Kaufman

WHILE SHEPHERDS WATCHED THEIR FLOCKS

Arr. by Steve Kaufman

105

1. While shepherds watch'd their flocks by night;
   All seated on the ground,
   The angel of the Lord came down,
   And glory shone around,
   And glory shone around.

2. "Fear not!" said he; for mighty dread
   Had seized their troubled mind,
   Glad tidings of great joy I bring
   To you and all mankind,
   To you and all mankind.

3. "To you, in David's town, this day
   Is born of David's line,
   The Savior who is Christ the Lord;
   And this shall be the sign,
   And this shall be the sign.

4. "The heavn'ly Babe you there shall find
   To human view display'd,
   All meanly wrapp'd in swathing bands,
   And in a manger laid.
   And in a manger laid."

POINTERS AND TIPS

Something I want to point out is that the songs in this book as with most of my books are not in any order other than semi-alphabetical. The last songs are not any harder than the first songs. So feel free to skip around throughout the book and play the songs that you like the best. Let's break down some of the harder, intermediate versions of the songs.

Be sure to play along with the recording. If there was no recording with this package, order it through Mel Bay Publications or by calling the author at 1-800-FLATPIK in the U.S. and 423-982-3808 outside the U.S. The recording is highly suggested for the intermediate/advanced versions.

Hark The Herald Angels Sing

You will notice many double stops in this arrangement as you will in many of these Christmas songs. The double stops are 2 notes that hit at the same time as if they were one. Be sure to hold the pressure down on the double stops to insure proper sustain.

Measures 6, 8, 10 and 12: Hammer on pull off triplets. Flick your finger onto the string and in a circular movement pull it back off again. Dig under the string for the pull-off part.

Measures 17 and 18 have some tricky sketches. Use the fingerings that are marked.

Silent Night

This arrangement is a bluesy sounding "Silent Night." I've put in a bunch of triplets to take up the slack of being a slow song that has many 2 and 3 beat melody notes. The best hints that I can give you for this arrangement is to count the triplets out **1-2-3 1-2-3 1-2-3**. Accent the "1" and don't stop once you've hit the first triplet.

Remember that all 1/8 notes by themselves should be hit with an **up swing**.

God Rest Ye Merry Gentlemen

This is a great minor mode song. The arrangement here is a lesson in running through minor riffs while still finding the melody notes along the way. It is very important in arranging solos that the melody is present.

Watch out for the 2 up swings in a row in measure 5.

Measure 10: There is a dot over the first note. Hit the D note loud but cut it off. It will have a staccato effect. Also, it gives you time to get to the next position and ready for the hammer-on. Use the fingerings marked.

Measure 17 uses the same hammer-on.

O Christmas Tree

This is another tune loaded with triplets and double stops. Remember to hold down the two notes of the double stops as long as possible to maximize the sustain. Some of the measures have a triplet that starts off with a hammer-on. Use the arrow markings as shown.

Measure 10 has a very quick hammer-on pull-off. They are 16th notes and sound like a trill. Hit them with a down swing then come up on the third fret note. To practice the timing of this action, play the 5th fret to the 3rd fret with a down up swing as if they were the only notes involved. Get used to how fast these **2** notes are played and then cram the other two notes in between them.

It Came Upon The Midnight Clear

Measure 1 to 2 has a hammer-on connecting the 2 measures. The hammer-on should be played slowly and then held out for the entire allotted time.

Measure 5 has an F note on the 3rd string that is to ring the entire measure while the notes on the 2nd string are played. This is difficult because in order to make this passage work you must leave the pressure on the 3rd string and work around the ringing note. Measure 6 is similar. Make it work.

Measures 9, 13, 17, 19, 25 and 29 have rolling sections which will sound the best if all fretted notes remain in place as long as possible. This will allow sustain and a nice ringing effect.

Go Tell It On The Mountain

This is a nice rolling arrangement. There should not be too much trouble in this version. The only difficulty that I can spot is in measure 13 where you'll find a double stop hammer-on. Have fun with this one and memorize (as with all of the arrangements) quickly.

The First Noël

Measure 3 has a difficult series of triplets. Normally you would hit the first note with a down swing and up on the starting note of each triplet. I find it easier to hit both notes per set with a down swing. This breaks the rule of right hand but I find it sounds and plays a little better this way. You can break the rule with slower songs but don't try it with the fast ones. You'll crash.

There is some good double stop work in measures 11, 12, 13, 14, 20, 21 and 22. The key to smooth sounding picking is sustain.

We Three Kings of Orient Are

The difficulty in this arrangement is in the holding of chord forms. You must hold the chord positions down and roll the right hand. Accent the first note of each chord roll. This is your melody note. Some of the fingerings are difficult. Take your time and memorize the arrangement.

O Come All Ye Faithful

Measures 2 and 8 are played with 16th note runs. It's hard to get the speed up but with the runs memorized and practiced correctly, you should be able to get these measures down in time for Christmas. The rest of the arrangement should not pose any difficulty.

In The Bleak Midwinter

This is my favorite tune in the book. My brother Mike suggested it and I owe him a thanks for that. I think it's my favorite because it's totally different than any other Christmas song that I've heard so far. It's a dark sounding tune and a lot of fun to play. There aren't too many songs that I like in the key of F!

Measures 2, 6 and 14 have hammer-on pull off triplets in them. Use your third and fourth finger for these triplets.

Measures 11 and 12: Have fun with these double stops and play 'em pretty.

Bring A Torch, Jeannette, Isabella

This is a light, swift moving three quarter timer. You shouldn't have any trouble picking through this one. Hold down the chord forms whenever possible. Memorize this song so you will be able to play it up to speed. Have fun with it!

Away In A Manger

This tune has two versions for you to work on. Measure 17 starts the variation. It has been arranged with symmetrics in mind. Notice the first three measures. They all have the same amount of musical syllables (da -da da da-da). The next measures with this same kind of "social significant value" can be found in the repeat of the same passage-measures 9-11. They all drone off of the A string. I bring this up because there needs to be thought involved in arrangements and not just stringing notes together. Find ways to arrange a song while still keeping the melody involved in the runs.

The variation is based on the same melody but one octave higher. I used triplets to get the melody out in front. Accent the first note of each triplet. You should see and hear how the triplets match in different segments of the arrangement—hopefully producing "Social Significant Value." Good luck and have fun!

Angels We Have Heard On High

There are not any tricky fingerings in this arrangement but there are a lot of notes and runs. The chorus plays melodic lines and runs through the chord changes. I had a lot of fun playing this piece for the recording and I'm sure you will enjoy playing it too. Good Luck!

What Child Is This?

This song is a special one to me. It is also known as "Greensleeves." I used it in the National Flatpicking Championships in 1984 and 1986 to help me win. I had not played it on the mandolin until I wrote this book and was pleased with the outcome.

There are many double stops in this arrangement. The double stops that are 2 beats or longer should be played with tremolo. Tremolo is played differently by all pickers. Just keep your count going while working on the tremolo. It is advised to play along with the recording. Other than making this slow song full of sustain and warm tone, you shouldn't have much trouble with the fingerings. Be sure to memorize this (and all) arrangements as soon as possible. You won't be able to watch your fingers and the page at the same time.

Deck The Halls

This is a flowing arrangement that is full of interchangeable runs. The runs are not too difficult. The difficulty lies in the speed. In order for this arrangement to sparkle it must be played quickly. Again, memorize this version because you need to watch your fingers and not the page.

Once in Royal David's City

This is another tune that was advised by my brother, Mike. Thanks again. There are many connecting runs involved here. Speed again is the issue for difficulty.

Measure 8 has a double stop hammer-on. Use the fingerings as they are marked. Be sure to attack the hammer-on. They need to have a lot of punch. Listen to the recording to hear what I mean.

O Little Town Of Bethlehem

Measure 2 is our first difficult spot. Hold the 2 finger C chord and hammer on the 3rd finger onto the 5th fret. The quarter notes give you a little time to switch position for the next hammer-on double stop. Be sure that when the hammer-on occurs that 2 notes can be heard. The same goes for measure 5.

Measures 11 and 12 consist of a long string of triplets. Follow the arrow markings. Each set of triplets will start with the opposite pick direction. They have to be played so quickly that if you start each set of triplets with a down swing that you may get out of time. Have fun with this arrangement.

Joy To The World

This is the only tune in this book in the key of E major. E is a fun key to play in because of the role of the 1st string "E." This arrangement utilizes the 1st string open. I use the 1st string like a drone as seen in measures 1, 2, 3, 9 and 11. Make sure not to bump a finger against this string so it can ring out along with the fretted notes.

The stretches in this song may be a bit harder than the other songs because of the 2nd, 4th and 6th fret runs.

Measures 15, 16 and 19 are tricky. Use the fingerings as they are marked. You must shift back in the middle of eighth note flurries. Slide your finger from the second fret to the first fret but hit (pick) all of the notes with the right hand. Watch out for the down ups and have fun with "Joy To The World".

Auld Lang Syne

Here is a fast one for you. It was great fun recording this one.

Measure 3: Accent the 1st, 3rd and 4th beats in this measure to make it sound more syncopated. Measure 8: Be sure to play this double stop hammer-on with power and clarity. Measures 11 and 15 have two up swings in a row between a slide. Make sure to let the slide last its full, allotted amount of time. Measure 21 has a position change on the open string. This will get you up to the 7th fret a little easier. Measure 29 has an eighth note hammer-on pull-off. Until now, we were using triplets for this action. Now they are eighth notes and you have to be sure not to rush the H.O./P.O. Practice along with the recording. If you have trouble keeping up with the recording, then listen to the arrangement a few dozen times.

The Golden Carol

This is a difficult tune to play because of the timing. It is our only 6/8 melody in this book. It moves along swiftly. One way to get the timing in your head is to count out **1** 2 3 4 5 6, **1** 2 3 4 5 6. Accent the 1st beat in every measure. This will help you keep track of where you are in the measure.

There are no real hard stretches or hard runs, when played slowly, but it's a hard song to play at tempo. Good Luck and have fun with this one.

Star In The East

This tune is played with a bounce or lilt. Instead of playing the eighth notes with straight time (like a sewing machine) play the 1st eighth note as a dotted eighth and the second eighth note as a sixteenth note. This will give you a Daa-Da Daa-Da Daa-Da Daa-Da effect. Long-short-long-short eighth notes.

Measure 1 and 5 have a sixteenth note H.O. P.O. Hit it with a down swing then come up on the last eighth note. In order to get used to the timing of this action, hit the first note tied together then the last note of the group. Down Up then hit the same 2 notes. Do this for a little while then cram the middle two notes in between them.

Measure 4 has a triplet with a hammer-on in it. Hit the first note down then hammer on the next note and finish the triplet with an up swing. Don't rush it–play it smoothly. Measures 7, 8 and 15 have the same actions.

The last measure is full of triplets. This case calls for you to hit them all. Alternate your down ups throughout the measure and you should be OK.

Down In Yon Forest

This is a great exercise in the key of Dm. The runs are not too difficult in this arrangement but you should notice which frets are frequently hit. They are like a pattern. Some of the 1st to 5th fret stretches are a little far but with time you'll play this song like a master. Good luck and memorize it quickly.

And The Trees Do Moan

This tune should pose no problem. It's another Dm tune but the chord structure is different than any other that I know. There are a few hammer ons and triplets but you ought to get right through this one.

While Shepherds Watched Their Flocks

Well you've made it to the last song of this collection. Congratulations! This last tune is very short but spunky. You shouldn't have any trouble playing this arrangement.

Good luck with all of the tunes in this collection and let me know how it goes. If you see me at a workshop, festival or concert somewhere be sure to come over and let me know how you did with this book as well as my other instructional materials. Remember, you can always call 1-800-FLATPIK in the U.S. and 423-982-3808 outside the U.S. with any questions. Also feel free to order my free "Flatpicking Hotline" newsletter and it will inform you with tips, songs, jokes and my whereabouts for workshops, concerts and festivals near you. Thanks again and see you soon – I hope.

STEVE KAUFMAN'S DISCOGRAPHY

The Arkansas Traveler – *Steve's newest flatpicking recording. 18 songs equaling 59 minutes and hot as a firecracker. Special guest Michele Voan sings 2 of the cuts. Steve sings 2 and picks 14 instrumentals.* **Available on CD only.**

To The Lady – *One of the most popular Steve Kaufman recordings. 58 minutes of hot fiddle tunes, ballads, 3 original instrumentals, 6 classic tunes. Lots of fun and great listening.* **Available on CD or long-playing cassette.**

Breaking Out – *Solo Steve Kaufman pickin'. "Whiskey Before Breakfast," "Jerusalem Ridge," "The I Miss You Waltz," "Temptation Rag," "Faded Love," "Turkey In The Straw" and more.* **58 minute CD or 38 minute Cassette.**

Star of the County Down – *A HOT duo recording with 1985 National Flatpicking Champ Robin Kessinger. "The World Is Waiting For The Sunrise," "Cattle In the Cane," "Calgary Polka" and more.* **Cassette only.**

Frost On The Window – *A remixed and remastered 44-minute cassette from 1985 with two new cuts. Six tunes were recorded as they were played in the National Flatpicking Championships. "Greensleeves," "New Camptown Races," "Red Wing," "Alabama Jubilee," "Grey Eagle," "Black and White Rag" plus 9 other selections.* **Cassette only.**

For Your Instructional Needs

A Smokey Mountain Christmas Book For Guitar with a 1-hour cassette – *24 Christmas classics for you to work on, sing with and enjoy for years to come. "In The Bleak Midwinter," "What Child Is This," "O Come All Ye Faithful" and more.* **Level: All.** *A full VHS video is also available.*

The Championship Flatpicking Guitar Book with a 1-hour cassette – *61 pages of* ***advanced*** *finger-burners. Some of the 16 tunes are: "Beaumont Rag," "Dill Pickle Rag," "Grey Eagle," "Sally Goodin."* **Level: Intermediate/Advanced.** *A full VHS video is also available.*

The Complete Flatpicking Guitar Book with a 1-hour cassette – *This book is for the* ***beginner*** *and is designed to take you all the way through the intermediate level to the edge of the advanced plane. 101 pages of tips and timesaving information. There are sections on bass walks, make arrangements to instrumentals and vocals, chord voicings, backup rhythm and brings you to the styles of Doc Watson, Norman Blake, Dan Crary, Tony Rice and Steve Kaufman.* **Level: Beginning/Intermediate.** *A compact disc and a full VHS video are also available.*

Flatpickin' The Gospels Book with a 1-hour cassette – *144+ pages of gospel songs for the Beginning-Advanced levels. This book teaches you to play the rhythm, a beginning melody, an intermediate/advanced melody and the words to 24 great songs.* **Level: All.** *A compact disc is also available. A VHS video for 14 of the most difficult arrangements is available.*

Power Flatpicking Book with a 1-hour cassette – *Learn to play in any key. Learn to play in any position or register. Unlock the mysteries of the bluegrass fingerboard and learn to be a "Power Flatpicker". You can throw away that capo now.* *A compact disc is also available.*

Bluegrass Guitar Solos That Every Parking Lot Picker Should Know Vol. 1 – *6 audio cassettes and a 165-page book of standard bluegrass Guitar Jamming Tunes written in notes and tablature. Learn to play: "Ragtime Annie," "Big Sandy River," "Bill Cheatham," "Billy In The Low Ground," "Gold Rush," "Double Eagle," "Flop-Eared Mule," "Fisher's Hornpipe," "Forked Deer," "Blackberry Blossom," "Old Joe Clark," "Turkey In The Straw," "Soldier's Joy," "St. Anne's Reel," "Nothing To It," "Arkansas Traveller," "Red-Haired Boy," "Sweet Georgia Brown," "Salt Creek" and "Whiskey Before Breakfast."* **Level: All.** *Also available for the mandolin.*

Bluegrass Guitar Solos That Every Parking Lot Picker Should Know Vol. 2 – *A sister series with the same format as Vol. 1. 6 cassettes with 20 more standard tunes for you to learn. You will learn to play: "Alabama Jubilee," "Black Mountain Rag," "Blackberry Rag," "Cherokee Shuffle," "Cricket On The Hearth," "Dixie Hoedown," "Down Yonder," "Eighth Of January," "John Hardy," "June Apple," "Katie Hill," "Liberty," "Mississippi Sawyer," "Peacock Rag," "Red Wing," "Stony Creek," "Temperance Reel," "Texas Gales," "Wheel Hoss" and, yes, "The Wildwood Flower."* **Level: All.**

Bluegrass Guitar Solos Every Parking Lot Picker Should Know Vol. 3 – *This is the same format as Volumes 1 and 2 except this series is designed to teach you to play the solos for 20 of the most standard bluegrass vocals. 115-page book with 6 cassettes.* **Level: All.**

Learning to Flatpick 2 - The Video – *A video produced for the beginner and intermediate level. Lots of tips and timesaving remedies to many of the mysteries of guitar picking. Some of the tunes covered in this 90-minute video are "The Wildwood Flower," "Old Joe Clark" and "Down Yonder."* **Level: Beginner/Intermediate.**

Learning to Flatpick 3 - The Video – *This has been developed for the intermediate/advanced player. Designed to help develop speed and style. Many tunes are broken down in this 90-minute video.* **Level: Intermediate/Advanced.**

Basic Bluegrass Rhythm - The Video – *This 70-minute video is designed to take the beginner to the band ready level of backup guitar. Steve will cover bass runs, fills, substitution chords and Texas style rhythm.* **Level: Beginner/Intermediate.**

Easy Gospel Guitar - The Video – *Through this 90-minute video, you will learn to* **play bluegrass/country guitar through your favorite gospel songs***. Whether you are a beginning or intermediate player, you will* **develop a repertoire** *of tunes and* **add style** *to songs you may already know. Steve slowly plays the accompaniment and melody of each song, then enhances the arrangement with* **basic chords, bass walks, hammer-ons, pull-offs, runs and other techniques***. You'll soon be playing wonderful arrangements to these well-known tunes: "Amazing Grace," "Just A Closer Walk With Thee," "Old-Time Religion," "The Old Rugged Cross," "Will The Circle Be Unbroken," "What A Friend We Have In Jesus" and "Cryin' Holy Unto The Lord."* **Level: Beginning/Intermediate.**

Steve Kaufman's 2 Hour Bluegrass Work Out (For All Instruments) - Series 1 and/or Series 2 – *designed as a practice tape, this series lets you play along with a band anytime at half speed or full speed. The lead is on the left speaker and the band is on the right speaker. There is very little instruction, the melodies are written in notes (tab for banjos) in a basic version. This way you can learn the simple melody and then jam with the tape. 2-One hour cassettes and book.* **Level: All -** *Specify instrument.*

You Can Teach Yourself® Flatpicking Guitar book with 1-hour cassette – *This book starts beginners out with their first two chords and takes you to high-end intermediate player. Also available on VHS video and CD.*

Steve Kaufman, P.O. Box 1020, Alcoa, TN. 37701 or call 1-800-FLATPIK (U.S.)
423-982-3808 (Outside U.S.) Voice or Fax